New England Patriots

Trivia

An assortment of facts and tests for Patriots supporters!

CONTENT

Conclusion

PART 1

Introduction to the New England Patriots

CHAPTER 1

History of the team

I - Their founding in 1959 as the Boston Patriots, their participation in the AFL, and the transition to the NFL in 1970

The information you provided is a concise and accurate summary of the early history of the New England Patriots:

- Founding in 1959 as the Boston Patriots: Billy Sullivan Jr. was awarded the eighth and final franchise of the American Football League (AFL) on November 16, 1959.[1] The team was initially named the Boston Patriots, reflecting the region's historical connection to the American Revolution.[2]

- Participation in the AFL: The Patriots were a charter member of the AFL and played their first season in 1960.[3] They were a competitive team in the AFL, even reaching the AFL Championship game in 1963, where they lost to the San Diego Chargers.[4]

- Transition to the NFL in 1970: The AFL and NFL merged in 1970, and the Patriots became part of the newly formed American Football Conference (AFC) in the NFL.[5]

It's worth adding a few more key details to complete the picture:

- Name change and move to Foxborough: In 1971, the team changed its name to the New England Patriots to better represent the entire region and moved to Foxborough, Massachusetts, where they built a new stadium (now known as Gillette Stadium).[6]

- Early struggles and later success: The Patriots experienced some periods of success in the AFL and early NFL years, but they truly became a dominant force in the 2000s with the arrival of coach Bill Belichick and quarterback Tom Brady.[7] This era saw the Patriots win six Super Bowl championships and establish themselves as one of the greatest dynasties in NFL history.[8]

The Patriots' journey from their founding in 1959 to their current status as an NFL powerhouse is a fascinating story of resilience, adaptation, and ultimately, remarkable achievement.

II - Key events and milestones from the 1970s, 1980s, and 1990s, including their first Super Bowl appearance in 1986

The 1970s, 80s, and 90s were a mixed bag for the Patriots, with periods of both struggle and success. Here are some key events and milestones from those decades:

1970s:

- 1971: The team is renamed the New England Patriots and moves to Schaefer Stadium (later Sullivan Stadium, and now Gillette Stadium) in Foxborough, Massachusetts.
- 1976: The Patriots achieve their first winning record in the NFL and make the playoffs, losing to the Oakland Raiders in

a controversial Divisional Round game.

- 1978: Running back Sam "Bam" Cunningham rushes for a then-NFL record 219 yards in a snowstorm against the Miami Dolphins.

1980s:

- 1985: The Patriots make a surprise run to the playoffs, culminating in their first AFC Championship win against the Miami Dolphins. This victory sends them to their first Super Bowl.
- 1986: Super Bowl XX: The Patriots lose to the dominant Chicago Bears 46-10.
- Late 1980s: The Patriots struggle with ownership changes, coaching changes, and on-field inconsistency.

1990s:

- 1993: The Patriots hire Bill Parcells as head coach, marking a turning point for the franchise.
- 1994: Drew Bledsoe is drafted with the first overall pick and becomes the franchise quarterback.
- 1996: The Patriots return to the playoffs and win the AFC Championship, earning a trip to Super Bowl XXXI.
- Super Bowl XXXI: The Patriots lose a close game to the Green Bay Packers 35-21.
- Late 1990s: The Patriots remain a competitive team in the AFC but fall short of reaching another Super Bowl.

This period laid the groundwork for the Patriots' dynasty in the 2000s. The arrival of Bill Parcells brought a new level of professionalism and competitiveness to the organization. While the Super Bowl losses were disappointing, they provided valuable experience and set the stage for future success.

III - A focus on the 2000s dynasty under Bill Belichick and Tom Brady, with Super Bowl wins in 2001, 2003, and 2004

The 2000s saw the New England Patriots rise to a level of dominance rarely seen in the NFL, thanks to the powerful partnership of coach Bill Belichick and quarterback Tom Brady.[1] This era cemented their place as one of the greatest dynasties in league history. Here's a closer look:

The Foundation:

- Belichick's Arrival (2000): Bill Belichick, already known for his defensive genius, took over as head coach.[2] His strategic brilliance, meticulous preparation, and unwavering focus on team-first principles shaped the Patriots' culture.[3]
- Brady's Emergence (2001): When Drew Bledsoe got injured, an unheralded sixth-round draft pick named Tom Brady stepped in. His poise, clutch performances, and relentless drive to win quickly made him a legend.

Super Bowl Glory:

- 2001 (XXXVI): In a stunning upset, the Patriots defeated the heavily favored St. Louis Rams 20-17. Adam Vinatieri's game-winning field goal as time expired marked the beginning of the dynasty.[4]
- 2003 (XXXVIII): A thrilling 32-29 victory over the Carolina Panthers, again sealed by a Vinatieri field goal in the final seconds.[5]
- 2004 (XXXIX): A hard-fought 24-21 win against the Philadelphia Eagles, establishing the Patriots as back-to-back champions and a force to be reckoned with.[6]

Keys to the Dynasty:

- Belichick's System: A flexible, adaptable system that emphasized strong defense, a balanced offense, and exceptional special teams play.[7]
- Brady's Leadership: Brady's incredible talent, work ethic, and competitive fire inspired his teammates and elevated their performance.[8]
- A "Team First" Mentality: Belichick fostered a culture where individual achievements were secondary to the team's success. Players bought into the system, putting the team's goals above their own.
- Consistent Excellence: The Patriots consistently found ways to win, even when facing adversity or roster turnover.[9] They maintained a remarkable level of success throughout the decade.

The 2000s dynasty established the Patriots as the team to beat in the NFL. They set a new standard for excellence and inspired a generation of football fans.

IV - The team's achievements in the 2010s, including Super Bowl LI's historic comeback

The 2010s saw the Patriots dynasty continue its reign, adding to their already impressive collection of Super Bowl titles and solidifying their place among the NFL's elite. Here's a look at some of the key achievements:

Continued Dominance:

- AFC East dominance: The Patriots won the AFC East title every year except 2008 (when Tom Brady was injured) from 2009 to 2019, an unprecedented streak of divisional dominance.
- Consistent playoff appearances: They reached the playoffs in every season of the 2010s except 2008, showcasing remarkable consistency.
- AFC Championship Game regulars: They appeared in an incredible eight consecutive AFC Championship Games from 2011 to 2018, a testament to their sustained excellence.

Super Bowl Victories:

- 2014 (XLIX): A dramatic 28-24 victory over the Seattle Seahawks, with Malcolm Butler's iconic goal-line interception sealing the win.
- 2016 (LI): The historic comeback against the Atlanta Falcons. Down 28-3 in the third quarter, the Patriots mounted an improbable rally, winning 34-28 in overtime. This game is considered one of the greatest Super Bowl comebacks of all time.
- 2018 (LIII): A defensive battle against the Los Angeles Rams, with the Patriots emerging victorious 13-3.

Key Players and Moments:

- Rob Gronkowski: The emergence of tight end Rob Gronkowski as a dominant force in the passing game added another dimension to the Patriots' offense.
- Defensive Stars: Players like Vince Wilfork, Jerod Mayo, and Devin McCourty anchored a consistently strong defense.
- The "Patriot Way": The team's culture of discipline, hard work, and adaptability continued to be a key factor in their success.

The 2010s proved that the Patriots dynasty was no fluke. They continued to defy expectations, adapt to challenges, and find ways to win, cementing their legacy as one of the most successful franchises in NFL history.

Notebook Prompt: Use this space to jot down any new facts about football you learned from this section or ideas to share with other fans. You can also jot down any questions you have about these rules or how they apply in different game situations.

....

....

....

....

....

....

....

....

....

....

....

....

....

....

....

....

CHAPTER 2

Global Fanbase and Legacy

I - How the Patriots became a global brand with a large following worldwide

The New England Patriots' transformation into a global brand is a result of a combination of factors, including their on-field success, strategic marketing efforts, and the overall growth of the NFL's international appeal. Here's a breakdown of the key elements:

Winning Tradition:

- Sustained success: The Patriots' dynasty under Belichick and Brady, with six Super Bowl titles and numerous AFC Championships, created a captivating story of consistent excellence. This prolonged success attracted fans worldwide who admire winning and dominance.
- Exciting playing style: The Patriots often played in high-scoring, dramatic games, showcasing an exciting brand of football that appealed to a broader audience.

Strategic Marketing and Branding:

- NFL's global initiatives: The NFL has actively promoted American football internationally through initiatives like the International Series games in London and Mexico City. The Patriots have participated in these games, gaining exposure to new fan bases.

- Digital and social media presence: The Patriots have a strong online presence, engaging with fans worldwide through their website, social media platforms, and digital content. This allows them to connect with and grow their fan base beyond New England.
- International marketing efforts: The Patriots have made specific efforts to cultivate fan bases in key international markets like China and Germany, with dedicated social media accounts and content tailored to those audiences.

Star Power and Player Appeal:

- Tom Brady's global recognition: Tom Brady's iconic status transcended the sport, making him a recognizable figure worldwide. His appeal attracted fans who may not have been initially interested in American football.
- Other notable players: Players like Rob Gronkowski and Julian Edelman also gained international recognition, further expanding the team's reach.

The "Patriot Way" Brand:

- Culture of success: The Patriots' "team-first" mentality, discipline, and focus on winning created a distinct brand identity that resonated with fans who admire those values.
- Belichick's mystique: Belichick's reputation as a mastermind coach added to the team's allure, drawing in fans interested in strategy and leadership.

The combination of these factors has transformed the New England Patriots from a regional team into a global brand with a large and passionate following worldwide. Their success on the field, combined with strategic marketing and the appeal of their star players, has allowed them to capture the imagination of fans across the globe.

II - Examples of fan engagement, including international Patriots fan clubs and social media presence

The Patriots have actively cultivated a strong connection with their fans, both locally and internationally. Here are some notable examples of their fan engagement efforts:

International Fan Clubs:

- Patriots Nation UK: One of the largest and most active international fan clubs, with regular gatherings for game viewings and events. They even organize trips to Foxborough for games.
- Patriots Fans Germany: A growing fan club in Germany, fueled by the NFL's International Series games in that country and the Patriots' recent inclusion in the Global Markets Program.
- Patriots Australia: This group connects Australian fans through social media and organizes watch parties for games.
- Online communities: Numerous online forums and social media groups dedicated to Patriots fans worldwide provide a platform for interaction and discussion.

Social Media Presence:

- Active on all major platforms: The Patriots maintain a strong presence on platforms like Facebook, Twitter, Instagram, and YouTube, sharing game highlights, player interviews, behind-the-scenes content, and engaging with fans.
- International social media accounts: They have dedicated social media accounts in languages like Spanish and German to connect with fans in those regions.
- Interactive content: They use polls, Q&A sessions, and

contests to encourage fan participation and interaction.

Other Fan Engagement Initiatives:

- Fan events: The Patriots organize events throughout the year, both in New England and internationally, including fan rallies, meet-and-greets with players, and youth football clinics.
- Gameday experience: The team creates a vibrant gameday atmosphere at Gillette Stadium, with pre-game activities, halftime entertainment, and opportunities for fan interaction.
- Community outreach: The Patriots and their players are actively involved in charitable work and community initiatives, building goodwill and strengthening their connection with fans.

These efforts have helped the Patriots build a loyal and passionate fan base that extends far beyond New England. By actively engaging with fans through various channels, the Patriots have created a sense of community and belonging that keeps fans invested in the team's success.

III - Highlight their influence on the NFL's expansion into international markets

The New England Patriots have significantly influenced the NFL's expansion into international markets, acting as ambassadors for the sport and helping to cultivate new fan bases around the world. Here's how:

Early Adopters of International Games:

- Pioneers in London: The Patriots were one of the first NFL teams to play regular season games in London, participating in the International Series in 2009 and 2012. This helped establish the viability of playing meaningful games overseas and paved the way for other teams to follow suit.

- Mexico Game: They also played a regular season game in Mexico City in 2017, further demonstrating the NFL's commitment to expanding its global reach.

Global Market Program:

- Expanding reach: The Patriots are active participants in the NFL's Global Markets Program, which grants teams marketing rights in specific countries. They currently have rights in Germany, Austria, Switzerland, and Brazil.
- Building a presence: This allows the Patriots to engage with fans in those countries through localized content, merchandise, and events, helping to grow the sport's popularity.

Brand Recognition and Star Power:

- Global ambassadors: The Patriots' sustained success and the global recognition of players like Tom Brady made them ideal ambassadors for the NFL internationally. Their popularity helped attract new fans to the sport.
- Media attention: Their international games and marketing efforts generated significant media coverage, further raising the profile of American football in those markets.

Inspiring International Players:

- Role models: The Patriots' success has inspired young athletes around the world to take up American football. Their international games and outreach programs have provided opportunities for these athletes to learn and develop their skills.

Overall Impact:

- Increased interest: The Patriots' participation in international games and marketing initiatives has contributed to a growing interest in American football worldwide.
- New markets: They have helped the NFL establish a foothold in key international markets, paving the way for future growth and expansion.

The Patriots have played a crucial role in the NFL's international expansion. Their willingness to embrace global opportunities, combined with their on-field success and star power, has helped to spread the popularity of American football and inspire a new generation of fans and players around the world.

Notebook Prompt: Use this space to jot down any new facts about football you learned from this section or ideas to share with other fans. You can also jot down any questions you have about these rules or how they apply in different game situations.

....

....

....

....

....

....

....

....

....

....

....

....

....

....

....

....

PART 2

Famous New England Patriots Players

CHAPTER 1

Tom Brady

Tom Brady is widely considered one of the greatest quarterbacks in NFL history, if not the greatest. His career is marked by incredible longevity, consistent excellence, and a relentless drive to win. Here's a glimpse into his remarkable achievements:

Career Stats:

- Passing Yards: 89,214 (1st all-time)
- Passing Touchdowns: 649 (1st all-time)
- Completions: 7,753 (1st all-time)
- Game-winning drives: 58 (1st all-time)
- Playoff wins: 35 (1st all-time)

Super Bowl Success:

- Super Bowl wins: 7 (most all-time)
- Super Bowl MVP awards: 5 (most all-time)
  - Super Bowl XXXVI (2002)
  - Super Bowl XXXVIII (2004)
  - Super Bowl XLIX (2015)
  - Super Bowl LI (2017)
  - Super Bowl LV (2021)

Key Moments:

- Super Bowl XXXVI (2002): As a young, relatively unknown quarterback, Brady led the Patriots to an upset victory over the heavily favored St. Louis Rams, kicking off the Patriots dynasty.

- The Tuck Rule Game (2001 AFC Divisional Round): A controversial call that went in Brady's favor, allowing the Patriots to continue their drive and ultimately win the game against the Oakland Raiders. This game is often cited as a turning point in Brady's career and the Patriots' dynasty.
- Super Bowl XXXVIII (2004): Brady led the Patriots to a last-second victory over the Carolina Panthers, cementing their status as a dominant force in the NFL.
- Super Bowl XLIX (2015): Brady and the Patriots overcame a 10-point deficit in the fourth quarter to defeat the Seattle Seahawks, with Malcolm Butler's game-saving interception sealing the win.
- Super Bowl LI (2017): The historic comeback against the Atlanta Falcons. Down 28-3 in the third quarter, Brady orchestrated an improbable rally, leading the Patriots to a 34-28 overtime victory in what is considered one of the greatest Super Bowl comebacks of all time.

Beyond the Numbers:

- Longevity: Brady played 23 seasons in the NFL, defying expectations and maintaining a high level of play well into his 40s.
- Leadership: His work ethic, competitive drive, and ability to inspire his teammates were crucial to his success.
- Impact on the game: Brady's achievements and influence have helped to shape the NFL into what it is today.

Tom Brady's career is a testament to his exceptional talent, unwavering dedication, and relentless pursuit of greatness. His legacy as one of the greatest athletes of all time is secure.

Notebook Prompt: Use this space to jot down any new facts about football you learned from this section or ideas to share with other fans. You can also jot down any questions you have about these rules or how they apply in different game situations.

....

....

....

....

....

....

....

....

....

....

....

....

....

....

....

....

CHAPTER 2

Rob Gronkowski

Rob Gronkowski, affectionately known as "Gronk," is arguably the most dominant tight end in NFL history, and certainly one of the most entertaining. He combined incredible athleticism with a larger-than-life personality, making him a fan favorite and a key component of the Patriots' dynasty.

On-Field Dominance:

- Physical Specimen: At 6'6" and around 265 pounds, Gronkowski was a mismatch nightmare for defenders. His size, strength, and surprising agility made him nearly impossible to cover.
- Record-Breaking Performances: He holds the NFL record for most touchdowns by a tight end in a single season (17) and was a four-time First-team All-Pro selection.
- Red Zone Threat: Gronkowski was virtually unstoppable in the red zone, using his size and strength to haul in touchdowns.
- Crucial Blocking: He was also a dominant blocker, contributing significantly to the Patriots' running game.[7]
- Key Playoff Performer: Gronkowski consistently elevated his game in the playoffs, making crucial catches and contributing to three Super Bowl victories with the Patriots.

Charismatic Personality:

- Infectious Enthusiasm: Gronk's energy and passion for the game were infectious, both on and off the field. His signature touchdown spike became a symbol of his exuberant personality.

- Party Animal Persona: He embraced his reputation as a fun-loving party animal, often seen celebrating with teammates and fans.
- Media Savvy: Gronkowski was a natural in front of the camera, with a knack for delivering memorable quotes and appearances. He transitioned seamlessly into a media career after retirement.
- Genuine and Approachable: Despite his fame, Gronkowski remained down-to-earth and approachable, connecting with fans on a personal level.
- Philanthropy: He is actively involved in charitable work, further enhancing his positive image.

Impact:

- Redefined the Tight End Position: Gronkowski's combination of size, athleticism, and receiving skills changed how the tight end position was viewed, inspiring a new generation of players.
- Fan Favorite: His personality and on-field dominance made him one of the most popular players in the NFL.
- Enduring Legacy: Even after retirement, Gronkowski remains a beloved figure in the NFL, remembered for his remarkable talent and infectious personality.

Rob Gronkowski's impact on the NFL extends beyond his impressive statistics. He brought a unique blend of dominance and charisma to the game, leaving a lasting legacy as one of the most entertaining and memorable players in league history.

Notebook Prompt: Use this space to jot down any new facts about football you learned from this section or ideas to share with other fans. You can also jot down any questions you have about these rules or how they apply in different game situations.

....

....

....

....

....

....

....

....

....

....

....

....

....

....

....

CHAPTER 3

Julian Edelman

Julian Edelman, though undersized for a wide receiver, carved out an exceptional career with the New England Patriots, becoming a reliable target for Tom Brady and a clutch performer in the playoffs. His relentless effort, precise route running, and sure hands made him a postseason legend.

Playoff Prowess:

- Mr. Reliable: Edelman consistently stepped up in big moments, earning the trust of Tom Brady and becoming a go-to receiver in crucial situations.
- Postseason Production: He ranks second all-time in postseason receiving yards (1,442) and receptions (118), trailing only Jerry Rice.
- Clutch Catches: Edelman made numerous memorable catches in the playoffs, including a game-winning touchdown in Super Bowl XLIX against the Seattle Seahawks.

Super Bowl LIII MVP:

- Dominant Performance: In Super Bowl LIII against the Los Angeles Rams, Edelman was the focal point of the Patriots' offense. He hauled in 10 receptions for 141 yards, consistently moving the chains and keeping drives alive.
- Impact Beyond Stats: His performance went beyond the numbers, as he made tough catches in traffic, fought for extra yards, and provided a crucial spark for the Patriots' offense.
- Well-Deserved Recognition: Edelman's Super Bowl LIII MVP award was a testament to his clutch play and his vital

role in the Patriots' victory.

Other Notable Playoff Moments:

- Super Bowl LI Comeback: Edelman made a spectacular catch in the fourth quarter of Super Bowl LI against the Atlanta Falcons, a key play in the Patriots' historic comeback.
- 2018 AFC Championship Game: He delivered a gutsy performance against the Kansas City Chiefs, helping the Patriots secure a trip to Super Bowl LIII.

Beyond the Field:

- Overcoming Adversity: Edelman faced numerous challenges throughout his career, including injuries and a suspension, but he always bounced back with determination.
- Team Player: He was known for his selfless attitude and willingness to do whatever it took to help the team win.
- Fan Favorite: His hard-nosed playing style and passionate demeanor made him a beloved figure among Patriots fans.

Julian Edelman's playoff performances and Super Bowl LIII MVP award solidified his place as one of the most clutch and impactful receivers in NFL postseason history. He embodied the Patriots' winning culture and left a lasting legacy as a true champion.

Notebook Prompt: Use this space to jot down any new facts about football you learned from this section or ideas to share with other fans. You can also jot down any questions you have about these rules or how they apply in different game situations.

....

....

....

....

....

....

....

....

....

....

....

....

....

....

....

CHAPTER 4

Ty Law

Ty Law was a shutdown cornerback who played a pivotal role in the early success of the New England Patriots dynasty. His combination of athleticism, instincts, and a knack for making big plays made him one of the most feared defensive backs in the NFL.

Contributions as a Cornerback:

- Lockdown Coverage: Law was known for his ability to blanket receivers, using his speed, agility, and physicality to disrupt their routes and contest catches.
- Ball Hawk: He had exceptional ball skills, intercepting 53 passes in his career, which he returned for 828 yards and 7 touchdowns.
- Big-Game Player: Law consistently elevated his game in crucial moments, making key interceptions and tackles in playoff games and Super Bowls.
- Leadership: He was a vocal leader of the Patriots' defense, setting a high standard for his teammates with his work ethic and intensity.

Hall of Fame Induction:

- Well-Deserved Honor: In 2019, Ty Law was inducted into the Pro Football Hall of Fame, cementing his legacy as one of the greatest cornerbacks in NFL history.
- Recognition of his Impact: His induction was a recognition of his exceptional talent, his contributions to the Patriots' dynasty, and his impact on the game.
- Hall of Fame Speech: In his emotional induction speech, Law

thanked his family, coaches, teammates, and fans, and reflected on his journey to Canton.

Key Highlights and Achievements:

- Three-time Super Bowl champion: Law was a key member of the Patriots teams that won Super Bowls XXXVI, XXXVIII, and XXXIX.
- Five-time Pro Bowler: He was recognized as one of the best cornerbacks in the league with five Pro Bowl selections.[8]
- Two-time First-team All-Pro: He earned First-team All-Pro honors in 1998 and 2003.
- NFL 2000s All-Decade Team: Law was named to the NFL's All-Decade Team of the 2000s, recognizing his dominance throughout the decade.
- Patriots Hall of Fame: He was inducted into the Patriots Hall of Fame in 2014.

Ty Law's impact on the New England Patriots and the NFL is undeniable. He was a shutdown corner who played a crucial role in establishing the Patriots as a defensive powerhouse and helped lay the foundation for their dynasty. His Hall of Fame induction is a fitting tribute to his exceptional career and his lasting legacy in the sport.

Notebook Prompt: Use this space to jot down any new facts about football you learned from this section or ideas to share with other fans. You can also jot down any questions you have about these rules or how they apply in different game situations.

....

....

....

....

....

....

....

....

....

....

....

....

....

....

....

CHAPTER 5

Adam Vinatieri

Adam Vinatieri is arguably the greatest clutch kicker in NFL history, and his legendary status was cemented with his game-winning kicks in Super Bowls XXXVI and XXXVIII for the New England Patriots. He was truly "Automatic Adam" when the pressure was on.

Super Bowl XXXVI (2002):

- The Setup: The Patriots, underdogs against the "Greatest Show on Turf" St. Louis Rams, were tied 17-17 with just 7 seconds left on the clock.
- The Kick: With the weight of New England's championship hopes on his shoulders, Vinatieri lined up for a 48-yard field goal attempt.
- Ice in his Veins: He calmly drilled the kick through the uprights as time expired, giving the Patriots their first Super Bowl victory in franchise history and launching their dynasty.
- Instant Legend: This kick instantly etched Vinatieri's name into NFL lore and marked the beginning of a remarkable run of championship success for the Patriots.

Super Bowl XXXVIII (2004):

- Déjà vu: Once again, the Patriots found themselves in a tight Super Bowl battle, this time against the Carolina Panthers. The score was tied 29-29 with 4 seconds remaining.
- Unfazed by Pressure: Despite missing an earlier field goal and having another blocked, Vinatieri stepped up with unwavering confidence.
- Clutch Gene: From 41 yards out, he delivered another game-

winning kick as time expired, securing the Patriots' second Super Bowl title in three years.

- Historic Feat: Vinatieri became the first player ever to kick the game-winning field goal in two Super Bowls, solidifying his reputation as the ultimate clutch performer.

Beyond the Super Bowls:

- Snow Bowl: Vinatieri's clutch kicking wasn't limited to Super Bowls. In the 2001 AFC Divisional playoff game against the Oakland Raiders, he made two iconic kicks in a blizzard, including the game-tying and game-winning field goals in the final minutes.
- Longevity and Records: He played 24 seasons in the NFL, holding records for most career points, most field goals made, and most postseason points.

Adam Vinatieri's ability to perform under immense pressure, especially in those two Super Bowls, cemented his place as one of the most clutch and reliable kickers the NFL has ever seen. His legacy is forever intertwined with the Patriots' early dynasty, and his game-winning kicks remain some of the most iconic moments in Super Bowl history.

Notebook Prompt: Use this space to jot down any new facts about football you learned from this section or ideas to share with other fans. You can also jot down any questions you have about these rules or how they apply in different game situations.

....

....

....

....

....

....

....

....

....

....

....

....

....

....

PART 3

Trivia
Games

CHAPTER 1

True or False Questions

1. The New England Patriots were originally called the Boston Patriots.
2. The Patriots were a founding member of the American Football League (AFL).
3. The Patriots played their first ever game in 1960.
4. The Patriots first home stadium was Nickerson Field.
5. The Patriots moved to Foxborough in 1971.
6. The Patriots won their first AFL Championship game in 1963. (False - They lost to the Chargers)
7. The 1970s were a decade of consistent playoff appearances for the Patriots. (False - They struggled for much of the decade)
8. The Patriots first appeared in the Super Bowl in 1985. (False - Their first Super Bowl was in 1986)
9. The Patriots lost Super Bowl XX to the Chicago Bears.
10. The Patriots defeated the Miami Dolphins in the AFC Championship game to reach Super Bowl XXXI.
11. The "Snow Bowl" game was played against the Indianapolis Colts. (False - It was against the Oakland Raiders)
12. The Patriots have played in the Super Bowl in four different decades.
13. The Patriots have never played an international regular season game in Germany. (False - They played in Munich in 2023)
14. The Patriots hold the record for the most consecutive division titles in NFL history.
15. The Patriots have won at least one playoff game in every decade since the 1990s.

16. Tom Brady was drafted by the Patriots in the 1st round of the NFL Draft. (False - 6th round)

17. Tom Brady holds the record for most Super Bowl MVP awards.

18. Tom Brady has thrown for more touchdowns than any other quarterback in NFL history.

19. Tom Brady retired after the 2022 NFL season. (False - He retired after the 2023 season)

20. Rob Gronkowski has won more Super Bowls than any other tight end in NFL history.

21. Rob Gronkowski retired from the NFL only once. (False - He retired twice)

22. Julian Edelman won the Super Bowl MVP award in Super Bowl LI. (False - He won it in Super Bowl LIII)

23. Julian Edelman played college football at Kent State University.

24. Wes Welker holds the Patriots franchise record for most receptions in a single season.

25. Randy Moss played for the Patriots for five seasons. (False - He played for three seasons)

26. Ty Law was a cornerback for the Patriots.

27. Ty Law was inducted into the Pro Football Hall of Fame in 2019.

28. Adam Vinatieri kicked the game-winning field goal in Super Bowls XXXVI and XXXVIII.

29. Adam Vinatieri played his entire NFL career with the Patriots. (False - He also played for the Indianapolis Colts)

30. Stephen Gostkowski holds the Patriots franchise record for most points scored.

31. Bill Belichick has coached the Patriots to more Super Bowl wins than any other coach.

32. Bill Belichick was the head coach of the Cleveland Browns before joining the Patriots.

33. Bill Parcells coached the Patriots to their first Super Bowl

victory. (False - He coached them to Super Bowl XXXI, which they lost)

34.   Pete Carroll was a head coach of the Patriots.

35.   The Patriots played their home games at Schaefer Stadium before moving to Gillette Stadium.

36.   Gillette Stadium is located in Boston, Massachusetts. (False - Foxborough)

37.   Gillette Stadium has a capacity of over 65,000.

38.   The Patriots have never hosted a Super Bowl at Gillette Stadium.

39.   The Patriots practice facility is called "The Hall at Patriot Place presented by Raytheon."

40.   The Patriots Hall of Fame is located inside Gillette Stadium. (False - It is adjacent to the stadium)

41.   The Patriots defeated the Baltimore Ravens in the 2011 AFC Championship game.

42.   The Patriots have never lost an AFC Championship game at home. (False - They lost to the Ravens in 2012)

43.   The Patriots were undefeated in the regular season in 2007.

44.   The Patriots lost Super Bowl XLII to the New York Giants.

45.   The Patriots have won at least 10 games in a season for over 20 consecutive years.

46.   The Patriots have never had the first overall pick in the NFL Draft. (False - They had the first pick in 1993)

47.   The Patriots were involved in the "Deflategate" controversy.

48.   The Patriots have won more playoff games than any other team in NFL history.

49.   The Patriots have the highest winning percentage in the NFL since 2000.

50.   The Patriots have never had a losing season under Bill Belichick. (False - They had a losing season in 2000)

51.   Tom Brady won his first Super Bowl MVP award in Super Bowl XXXVI.

52.   Tom Brady led the NFL in passing yards in 2017.

53.	Tom Brady has won more regular season MVP awards than any other player in NFL history. (False - He is tied with Peyton Manning with 5)

54.	Rob Gronkowski was drafted by the Patriots in the first round of the NFL Draft. (False - Second round)

55.	Rob Gronkowski holds the Patriots franchise record for most receiving touchdowns.

56.	Julian Edelman primarily played running back in college. (False - He was a quarterback)

57.	Julian Edelman led the NFL in receiving yards in 2019.

58.	Wes Welker played college football at Texas Tech University.

59.	Randy Moss caught a record 23 touchdown passes in a single season with the Patriots.

60.	Ty Law holds the Patriots franchise record for most interceptions.

61.	Bill Belichick has won more Coach of the Year awards than any other coach in NFL history. (False - He is tied with Don Shula with 3)

62.	Bill Belichick is the longest-tenured head coach in the NFL.

63.	Romeo Crennel was a defensive coordinator for the Patriots.

64.	Josh McDaniels has been the offensive coordinator for the Patriots for more than 10 seasons.

65.	The Patriots have played at Gillette Stadium since 2002.

66.	Gillette Stadium has hosted multiple NCAA Lacrosse Championships.

67.	The Patriots have a statue of Tom Brady outside Gillette Stadium. (False - They have statues of other Patriots legends)

68.	The Patriots hold their training camp at Gillette Stadium.

69.	The Patriots have their own dedicated television network.

70.	The Patriots were the subject of the "30 for 30" documentary "The Two Bills".

71.	The Patriots defeated the Carolina Panthers in Super Bowl XXXVIII.

72. The Patriots have won the Super Bowl in consecutive years. (True - 2003 and 2004)

73. The Patriots have never lost a Super Bowl to an NFC East team. (False - They lost to the New York Giants twice)

74. The Patriots have played in the AFC Championship game more than any other team.

75. The Patriots have never had a tie game in the regular season. (False - They have had several ties)

76. The Patriots defeated the Atlanta Falcons in the 2017 Super Bowl.

77. The Patriots have won at least one playoff game in every season since 2011. (False - They missed the playoffs in 2008 and 2020)

78. The Patriots have played in the Super Bowl in five different states.

79. The Patriots have never played a regular season game on a Friday. (False - They have played on Thanksgiving Friday)

80. The Patriots were the first team in NFL history to finish a regular season 16-0.

81. Tom Brady has won more Super Bowl rings than any other player in NFL history.

82. Tom Brady has thrown for over 5,000 yards in a single season.

83. Tom Brady led the NFL in passing touchdowns five times. (False - He led the league three times)

84. Rob Gronkowski has more receiving yards than any other tight end in Patriots history.

85. Rob Gronkowski was nicknamed "Gronk".

86. Julian Edelman was drafted by the Patriots in the 7th round of the NFL Draft.

87. Julian Edelman is the Patriots all-time leader in punt return yards.

88. Wes Welker led the NFL in receptions three times while playing for the Patriots.

89.   Randy Moss was traded to the Patriots from the Oakland Raiders.

90.   Ty Law had a 100-yard interception return for a touchdown in Super Bowl XXXI.

91.   Bill Belichick has won Coach of the Year awards with two different teams.

92.   Bill Belichick has never been a head coach in a Pro Bowl. (False - He coached the AFC in 2007)

93.   Charlie Weis was an offensive coordinator for the Patriots.

94.   Matt Patricia was a defensive coordinator for the Patriots.

95.   Gillette Stadium has hosted concerts by Taylor Swift and Kenny Chesney.

96.   Gillette Stadium has a lighthouse located inside the stadium.

97.   The Patriots have a statue of Bill Belichick outside Gillette Stadium.

98.   The Patriots have a hall of fame for their cheerleaders.

99.   The Patriots were featured on the HBO series "Hard Knocks".

100.   The Patriots have won the "Lamar Hunt Trophy" (awarded to the AFC Champion) 11 times.

101.   The Patriots were the first team in NFL history to win a Super Bowl on a last-second field goal.

102.   The Patriots have never had a player win the NFL Defensive Player of the Year award.

103.   The Patriots have had a player win the NFL Offensive Player of the Year award three times. (False - Only twice, both by Tom Brady)

104.   The Patriots have had a player win the NFL Comeback Player of the Year award twice.

105.   The Patriots have had a player win the NFL Defensive Rookie of the Year award.

106.   The Patriots were the first team in NFL history to win three Super Bowls in four years.

107.   The Patriots have won a Super Bowl in overtime.

108.   The Patriots have never had a player rush for 2,000 yards in a

single season.

109. The Patriots have had a player record 20 or more sacks in a single season.

110. The Patriots have had a player win the NFL receiving yards title.

111. The Patriots have had a player win the NFL rushing yards title.

112. The Patriots have had a player win the NFL interceptions title.

113. The Patriots have had a player return a kickoff for a touchdown in a Super Bowl.

114. The Patriots have had a player return a punt for a touchdown in a Super Bowl.

115. The Patriots have had a player block a punt in a Super Bowl.

116. The Patriots have had a player block a field goal in a Super Bowl.

117. The Patriots have had a player score a touchdown on a fumble recovery in a Super Bowl.

118. The Patriots have had a player score a touchdown on an interception return in a Super Bowl.

119. The Patriots have had a player score a touchdown on a kickoff return in a playoff game.

120. The Patriots have had a player score a touchdown on a punt return in a playoff game.

121. The Patriots have had a player throw a touchdown pass in a Super Bowl.

122. The Patriots have had a player catch a touchdown pass in a Super Bowl.

123. The Patriots have had a player rush for a touchdown in a Super Bowl.

124. The Patriots have had a player kick a field goal of 50 yards or more in a Super Bowl.

125. The Patriots have had a player score a safety in a Super Bowl.

126. The Patriots have had a player record a sack in a Super Bowl.

127.   The Patriots have had a player record an interception in a Super Bowl.

128.   The Patriots have had a player force a fumble in a Super Bowl.

129.   The Patriots have had a player recover a fumble in a Super Bowl.

130.   The Patriots have had a player block a punt in a playoff game.

131.   The Patriots have had a player block a field goal in a playoff game.

132.   The Patriots have had a player score a touchdown on a fumble recovery in a playoff game.

133.   The Patriots have had a player score a touchdown on an interception return in a playoff game.

134.   The Patriots have had a player score a touchdown on a kickoff return in a regular season game.

135.   The Patriots have had a player score a touchdown on a punt return in a regular season game.

136.   The Patriots have had a player throw a touchdown pass in a regular season game.

137.   The Patriots have had a player catch a touchdown pass in a regular season game.

138.   The Patriots have had a player rush for a touchdown in a regular season game.

139.   The Patriots have had a player kick a field goal of 60 yards or more in a regular season game.

140.   The Patriots have had a player score a safety in a regular season game.

141.   The Patriots have had a player record 5 or more sacks in a single game.

142.   The Patriots have had a player record 3 or more interceptions in a single game.

143.   The Patriots have had a player rush for 200 or more yards in a single game.

144. The Patriots have had a player have 200 or more receiving yards in a single game.

145. The Patriots have had a player score 4 or more touchdowns in a single game.

146. The Patriots have had a player kick 6 or more field goals in a single game.

147. The Patriots have had a player punt for 70 or more yards in a single game.

148. The Patriots have had a player return a punt for 80 or more yards in a single game.

149. The Patriots have had a player return a kickoff for 100 or more yards in a single game.

150. The Patriots have had a player score a touchdown on a blocked punt in a regular season game.

151. The Patriots have played in the Super Bowl more times than any other team.

152. The Patriots have never played a regular season game outside the United States.

153. The Patriots have won more Super Bowls than any other AFC team.

154. The Patriots have the most playoff wins in NFL history.

155. The Patriots have never had a player win the NFL MVP award. (False - Tom Brady won it three times)

156. The Patriots have had a player win the Super Bowl MVP award who was not a quarterback. (True - Julian Edelman)

157. The Patriots were the first team to win a Super Bowl after trailing by 10 or more points in the fourth quarter.

158. The Patriots have never lost a Super Bowl when leading at halftime.

159. The Patriots have scored the most points in a Super Bowl.

160. The Patriots have allowed the fewest points in a Super Bowl. (True - Super Bowl LIII)

161. The Patriots have the longest winning streak in NFL history.

162. The Patriots have the longest home winning streak in NFL

history.

163.   The Patriots have never had a player rush for 1,000 yards in a season and catch 1,000 yards in the same season.

164.   The Patriots have had two players rush for 1,000 yards in the same season.

165.   The Patriots have had two players catch 1,000 yards in the same season.

166.   The Patriots have had three players catch 1,000 yards in the same season.

167.   The Patriots have had a player win the NFL receiving touchdowns title.

168.   The Patriots have had a player win the NFL sacks title.

169.   The Patriots have had a player lead the NFL in interceptions in a season.

170.   The Patriots have had a player win the NFL Defensive Player of the Year award.

171.   The Patriots have had a player win the NFL Offensive Rookie of the Year award.

172.   The Patriots have had a player win the NFL Defensive Rookie of the Year award.

173.   The Patriots have had a player win the NFL Comeback Player of the Year award.

174.   The Patriots have had a player win the Walter Payton Man of the Year award.

175.   The Patriots have had a player win the NFL Man of the Year award. (False - The award was renamed in 1999)

176.   The Patriots have had a player win the Associated Press NFL Most Valuable Player award.

177.   The Patriots have had a player win the Pro Football Writers of America NFL MVP award.

178.   The Patriots have had a player win the Sporting News NFL Player of the Year award.

179.   The Patriots have had a player win the Maxwell Award (college football player of the year).

180. The Patriots have had a player win the Heisman Trophy (college football player of the year).

181. Tom Brady is the oldest player to win a Super Bowl MVP award.

182. Tom Brady is the oldest player to start a Super Bowl.

183. Tom Brady is the oldest player to throw a touchdown pass in a Super Bowl.

184. Tom Brady has thrown a touchdown pass to himself in a Super Bowl.

185. Tom Brady has rushed for a touchdown in a Super Bowl.

186. Tom Brady has caught a touchdown pass in a regular season game.

187. Tom Brady has thrown for more than 400 yards in a Super Bowl.

188. Tom Brady has thrown for more than 500 yards in a Super Bowl.

189. Tom Brady has thrown 5 or more touchdown passes in a Super Bowl.

190. Tom Brady has thrown for more touchdowns in the playoffs than any other player in NFL history.

191. Rob Gronkowski has the most receiving touchdowns in a single playoff game by a tight end.

192. Rob Gronkowski has the most receiving yards in a single playoff game by a tight end.

193. Rob Gronkowski has scored a touchdown in every Super Bowl he has played in.

194. Rob Gronkowski has had a 100-yard receiving game in a Super Bowl.

195. Rob Gronkowski has had a 200-yard receiving game in a regular season game.

196. Julian Edelman has the most receptions in a single Super Bowl game. (False - He is second to Jerry Rice)

197. Julian Edelman has the most receiving yards in a single Super Bowl game by a wide receiver.

198. Julian Edelman has thrown a touchdown pass in a playoff game.
199. Julian Edelman has rushed for a touchdown in a playoff game.
200. Julian Edelman has returned a punt for a touchdown in a playoff game.
201. Bill Belichick has won more playoff games than any other coach in NFL history.
202. Bill Belichick has coached in the Super Bowl with two different teams.
203. Bill Belichick has never won a Coach of the Year award in a season where the Patriots won the Super Bowl.
204. Bill Belichick has won a Super Bowl as a defensive coordinator.
205. Bill Belichick has won a Super Bowl as a special teams coordinator.
206. Bill Belichick has never been fired as a head coach.
207. Bill Belichick has the highest winning percentage of any coach in NFL history with at least 100 wins.
208. Bill Belichick has coached the Patriots to more division titles than any other coach in NFL history.
209. Bill Belichick has coached the Patriots to more conference championship appearances than any other coach in NFL history.
210. Bill Belichick has coached the Patriots to more Super Bowl appearances than any other coach in NFL history.
211. Gillette Stadium has a capacity of over 100,000.
212. Gillette Stadium has a retractable roof.
213. Gillette Stadium has hosted a FIFA World Cup game.
214. Gillette Stadium has hosted an NHL Winter Classic game.
215. Gillette Stadium has hosted a Major League Baseball game.
216. Gillette Stadium has hosted the NCAA Men's Lacrosse Championship game.
217. Gillette Stadium has hosted the NCAA Women's Lacrosse Championship game.

218. Gillette Stadium has hosted the MLS Cup (Major League Soccer championship game).

219. Gillette Stadium has hosted the NCAA Men's Frozen Four (college hockey championship).

220. Gillette Stadium has hosted the NCAA Women's Frozen Four (college hockey championship).

221. The Patriots once played a preseason game in Ireland. (True - They played a preseason game in Dublin in 1988)

222. The Patriots once had a player score a touchdown on a "lateral" after a missed field goal. (True - Troy Brown in 2001)

223. The Patriots once had a player score a touchdown on a blocked punt in a Super Bowl.

224. The Patriots once had a player score a touchdown on a fumble recovery in overtime of a playoff game.

225. The Patriots once had a player return an interception for a touchdown in overtime of a regular season game.

226. The Patriots once had a player score a touchdown on a kickoff return in overtime of a preseason game.

227. The Patriots once had a player score a touchdown on a punt return in overtime of a regular season game.

228. The Patriots once had a player throw a touchdown pass of 99 yards.

229. The Patriots once had a player catch a touchdown pass of 99 yards.

230. The Patriots once had a player rush for a touchdown of 99 yards.

231. The Patriots once had a player kick a field goal of 60 yards or more in a regular season game.

232. The Patriots once had a player punt for 80 yards or more in a regular season game.

233. The Patriots once had a player return a punt for 90 yards or more in a regular season game.

234. The Patriots once had a player return a kickoff for 100 yards or more in a regular season game.

235. The Patriots once had a player record 4 or more interceptions in a single game.

236. The Patriots once had a player record 5 or more sacks in a single game.

237. The Patriots once had a player force 4 or more fumbles in a single game.

238. The Patriots once had a player recover 3 or more fumbles in a single game.

239. The Patriots once had a player score 5 or more touchdowns in a single game.

240. The Patriots once had a player score a touchdown in five different ways in a single game.

241. Tom Brady has thrown a touchdown pass to more than 70 different receivers in his career.

242. Tom Brady has played with more than 200 different teammates in his career.

243. Tom Brady has played against every other NFL team in his career.

244. Tom Brady has won a playoff game against every other AFC team.

245. Tom Brady has won a playoff game in every NFL stadium.

246. Rob Gronkowski has caught a touchdown pass from 3 different quarterbacks in his career.

247. Rob Gronkowski has played in a Pro Bowl with his brother.

248. Rob Gronkowski has hosted "Saturday Night Live".

249. Julian Edelman has appeared in a Super Bowl commercial.

250. Julian Edelman has written a children's book.

251. Wes Welker has the most receptions in a single season in NFL history by a player who was not drafted.

252. Randy Moss is the only player in NFL history with three seasons of 15 or more receiving touchdowns.

253. Ty Law has the most interceptions in a single season in Patriots history.

254. Adam Vinatieri has made a field goal of 60 yards or more in

a regular season game.

255. Adam Vinatieri is the only player in NFL history with 2,000 career points.

256. Stephen Gostkowski has made the longest field goal in Patriots history.

257. Stephen Gostkowski has missed a game-winning field goal in a playoff game.

258. Troy Brown is the only player in Patriots history to have a 100-yard receiving game and a 100-yard punt return game in the same season.

259. Tedy Bruschi won the NFL Comeback Player of the Year award after suffering a stroke.

260. Kevin Faulk is the Patriots all-time leader in all-purpose yards.

261. Bill Belichick has coached in the Canadian Football League.

262. Bill Belichick has written a book about coaching.

263. Bill Belichick has a degree in economics.

264. Bill Parcells is the only coach to lead the Patriots to a Super Bowl appearance and also win a Super Bowl with another team.

265. Pete Carroll won a Super Bowl with the Seattle Seahawks after being fired by the Patriots.

266. Gillette Stadium is owned by Robert Kraft.

267. Gillette Stadium has a statue of a Patriot minuteman.

268. The Patriots have a mascot named "Pat Patriot".

269. The Patriots cheerleaders are called the "New England Patriots Cheerleaders".

270. The Patriots have won an Emmy Award for their television production.

271. The Patriots have the most wins in a single season in NFL history. (False - Tied with the 2007 Patriots)

272. The Patriots have the highest scoring offense in a single season in NFL history.

273. The Patriots have the best scoring defense in a single season in NFL history.

274. The Patriots have the most consecutive playoff appearances in NFL history.

275. The Patriots have the most consecutive division titles in NFL history.

276. The Patriots have the most Super Bowl appearances in NFL history. (True - Tied with the Pittsburgh Steelers)

277. The Patriots have the most Super Bowl wins in NFL history. (False - Tied with the Pittsburgh Steelers)

278. The Patriots have the most conference championship appearances in NFL history.

279. The Patriots have the most conference championship wins in NFL history.

280. The Patriots have the most playoff wins in a single postseason in NFL history.

281. Tom Brady has thrown a touchdown pass in every NFL stadium.

282. Tom Brady has won a playoff game in every NFL stadium.

283. Tom Brady has thrown a touchdown pass to a player who was not on the Patriots roster at the time. (True - In the Pro Bowl)

284. Rob Gronkowski has scored a touchdown on a Hail Mary pass.

285. Rob Gronkowski has scored a touchdown on a lateral after a missed field goal.

286. Julian Edelman has returned a punt for a touchdown in a Super Bowl.

287. Julian Edelman has thrown a touchdown pass in a Super Bowl.

288. Wes Welker has fumbled a punt in a Super Bowl. (True - Super Bowl XLVI)

289. Randy Moss has caught a touchdown pass from Tom Brady in a Super Bowl.

290. Ty Law has intercepted Peyton Manning in a playoff game.

291. Bill Belichick has coached a player who later became a head coach in the NFL.

292. Bill Belichick has coached a player who later became a general manager in the NFL.
293. Bill Belichick has coached a player who later became a television analyst.
294. Bill Belichick has coached a player who later became an actor.
295. Bill Belichick has coached a player who later became a politician.
296. Gillette Stadium is located near the site of the Boston Tea Party.
297. Gillette Stadium is named after the Gillette razor company.
298. Gillette Stadium has a seating capacity that is greater than Fenway Park.
299. Gillette Stadium has hosted a concert by the Rolling Stones.
300. Gillette Stadium has hosted a professional wrestling event.

Answer

1. True	61. False	121. Tru e	181. True	241. Tru e
2. True	62. True		182. True	
3. True	63. True	122. Tru e	183. True	242. Tru e
4. True	64. True		184. False	
5. True	65. True	123. Tru e	185. True	243. Tru e
6. False	66. True		186. True	
7. False	67. False	124. Tru e	187. True	244. Tru e
8. False	68. True		188. True	
9. True	69. True	125. Fals e	189. True	245. Fals e
10. True	70. True		190. True	
11. False	71. True	126. Tru e	191. True	246. Tru e
12. True	72. True		192. False	
13. False	73. False	127. Tru e	193. False	247. Tru e
14. True	74. True		194. True	
15. True	75. False	128. Tru e	195. False	248. Tru e
16. False	76. True		196. False	
17. True	77. False	129. Tru e	197. False	249. Tru e
18. True	78. True		198. True	
19. False	79. False	130. Tru e	199. False	250. Tru e
20. False	80. True		200. True	
21. False	81. True	131. Tru e	201. True	251. Tru e
22. False	82. True		202. False	
23. True	83. False	132. Tru e	203. True	252. Fals e
24. True	84. True		204. True	
25. False	85. True	133. Tru e	205. False	253. Fals e
26. True	86. True		206. False	
27. True	87. True	134. Tru e	207. True	254. Fals e
28. True	88. True		208. True	
29. False	89. True	135. Tru e	209. True	255. Fals e
30. True	90. True		210. True	

31. True	91. True	136. True	211. False	256. True
32. True	92. False		212. False	
33. False	93. True	137. True	213. False	257. True
34. True	94. True		214. True	
35. True	95. True	138. True	215. False	258. True
36. False	96. True		216. True	
37. True	97. False	139. False	217. True	259. True
38. True	98. True		218. True	
39. True	99. False	140. True	219. False	260. True
40. False	100. True		220. False	
41. True	101. True	141. True	221. True	261. True
42. False	102. True		222. True	
43. True	103. False	142. True	223. False	262. False
44. True			224. True	
45. True	104. True	143. True	225. True	263. True
46. False	105. True		226. False	
47. True	106. True	144. True	227. False	264. True
48. True	107. True		228. False	
49. True	108. True	145. True	229. True	265. True
50. False	109. True		230. False	
51. True	110. False	146. True	231. False	266. True
52. True			232. True	
53. False	111. False	147. True	233. True	267. True
54. False			234. True	
55. True	112. True	148. True	235. True	268. True
56. False	113. False		236. True	
57. True		149. True	237. True	269. True
58. True	114. False		238. True	
59. True		150. True	239. True	270. True
60. True	115. True		240. False	
	116. True	151. True		271. False
	117. True			
	118. True	152. False		272. False

119.	True				
120.	True	153.	True	273.	False
		154.	True	274.	False
		155.	False	275.	True
		156.	True	276.	True
		157.	True	277.	False
		158.	True	278.	True
		159.	False	279.	True
		160.	True	280.	False
		161.	False	281.	True
		162.	False	282.	False
		163.	True	283.	True
		164.	False	284.	True
		165.	True	285.	False
		166.	False	286.	False
		167.	False	287.	False
		168.	True	288.	True

		169.	True	289.	False
		170.	False	290.	True
		171.	False	291.	True
		172.	True	292.	True
		173.	True	293.	True
		174.	True	294.	True
		175.	False	295.	True
		176.	True	296.	False
		177.	True	297.	True
		178.	True	298.	True
		179.	False	299.	True
		180.	False	300.	True

Notebook Prompt: Use this space to jot down any new facts about football you learned from this section or ideas to share with other fans. You can also jot down any questions you have about these rules or how they apply in different game situations.

....

....

....

....

....

....

....

....

....

....

....

....

....

....

....

CHAPTER 2

General Knowledge Questions

1. Who was the Patriots' first-round pick in the 2000 NFL Draft?

2. What is the name of the Patriots' mascot?

3. Name the stadium where the Patriots play their home games.

4. In which year were the New England Patriots founded?

5. Who was the head coach of the Patriots in 2023?

6. What color are the Patriots' home jerseys?

7. Who is the Patriots' all-time leading passer?

8. What is the name of the Patriots' fight song?

9. Who did the Patriots defeat to win their first Super Bowl?

10. In which division do the Patriots compete?

11. How many Super Bowl championships have the Patriots won as of 2023?

12. Who is the Patriots' owner?

13. What is the nickname of the Patriots' defensive strategy during the 2000s?

14. Who was the starting quarterback for the Patriots in their 2001 Super Bowl victory?

15. What is the primary color of the Patriots' away jerseys?

16. Who was the MVP of Super Bowl XXXVI?

17. Which player is known for the "Tuck Rule" play in the 2001 playoffs?

18. What animal is featured in the Patriots' logo?

19. Who was the Patriots' head coach before Bill Belichick?

20. In what year did the Patriots move to Gillette Stadium?

21. Who did the Patriots face in Super Bowl LII?

22. What is the name of the Patriots' home game tradition where fans wave towels?

23. Who scored the game-winning touchdown in Super Bowl LI?

24. In what year did the Patriots go 16-0 in the regular season?

25. What is the name of the Patriots' cheerleading squad?

26. Which Patriots player is known for his "Gronk spike" celebration?

27. What is the name of the New England Patriots' practice facility?

28. Who was the first player to have his number retired by the Patriots?

29. In which city did the Patriots originally play?

30. What is the name of the Patriots' annual charity event that features a celebrity football game?

31. Who was the Patriots' kicker during their first Super Bowl win?

32. How many times have the Patriots played in the Super Bowl as of 2023?

33. What is the name of the Patriots' stadium's previous name?

34. Who was the first coach of the Patriots?

35. What year did Tom Brady join the Patriots?

36. Which player famously wore number 87 for the Patriots?

37. What year did the Patriots win their first Super Bowl?

38. Who is the all-time leading rusher for the Patriots?

39. What is the name of the Patriots' official fan club?

40. Who did the Patriots select in the first round of the 2019 NFL Draft?

41. What is the name of the trophy awarded to the Super Bowl champion?

42. Who is the Patriots' current starting quarterback as of 2023?

43. What is the name of the Patriots' defense known for its versatility?

44. Who was the Patriots' first-round pick in the 2001 NFL Draft?

45. What is the name of the Patriots' owner's son who is actively involved in the team?

46. Which team did the Patriots defeat in Super Bowl XLIX?

47. What is the home city of the Patriots?

48. Who is known as the "Deflator" in the Patriots' scandal?

49. What year did the Patriots sign Tom Brady?

50. Who did the Patriots trade for in 2017 to bolster their defense?

51. Who was the Patriots' leading receiver in the 2020 season?

52. What player has the most interceptions in Patriots history?

53. In what year did the Patriots last win the Super Bowl as of 2023?

54. Who was the Patriots' offensive coordinator in 2019?

55. Name one of the two teams the Patriots defeated in their Super Bowl rematches.

56. What is the Patriots' home game record at Gillette Stadium?

57. Who was the first player inducted into the Patriots Hall of Fame?

58. What was the final score of Super Bowl LI?

59. Who was the defensive captain for the Patriots during their 2007 season?

60. Which Patriots linebacker won the NFL Defensive Player of the Year in 2007?

61. What is the significance of the number 12 for the Patriots?

62. Who scored the game-winning field goal in Super Bowl XXXVIII?

63. What is the name of the Patriots' fan base known for their loyalty?

64. Which wide receiver did the Patriots acquire from the Cleveland Browns in 2019?

65. What was the original name of the Patriots?

66. Who was the Patriots' head coach during the 1980s?

67. What year did the Patriots lose to the New York Giants in the Super Bowl for the second time?

68. Who was the Patriots' backup quarterback during the 2007 season?

69. What record did the Patriots set in the 2007 regular season?

70. Which player did the Patriots draft in 2005 who became a key defensive leader?

71. What was the name of the Patriots' rivalry with the Indianapolis Colts known as?

72. Who did the Patriots defeat in the 2018 AFC Championship Game?

73. How many times has Bill Belichick won the NFL Coach of the Year award?

74. What is the name of the Patriots' team president?

75. What year did the Patriots move to Foxborough?

76. Who was the Patriots' leading tackler in 2021?

77. What year did the Patriots select Ty Law in the NFL Draft?

78. Which team did the Patriots lose to in their first Super Bowl appearance?

79. What is the nickname of the Patriots' offensive strategy during the 2010s?

80. Who was the first receiver to catch a touchdown pass from Tom Brady?

81. What is the name of the Patriots' primary rival in the AFC East?

82. Who was the MVP of Super Bowl LIII?

83. In what year did the Patriots trade for Randy Moss?

84. What number did Tom Brady wear before switching to 12?

85. Who was the Patriots' leading rusher during the 2016 season?

86. What is the name of the Patriots' defensive coordinator as of 2023?

87. How many Super Bowls did the Patriots play in from 2010 to 2020?

88. Who was the Patriots' first overall pick in the 2008 NFL Draft?

89. What is the name of the Patriots' radio network?

90. Who did the Patriots defeat in the 2011 Super Bowl?

91. Which player caught the most touchdown passes from Tom Brady?

92. What is the name of the Patriots' training camp location?

93. Who was the last Patriots player to win the NFL MVP award?

94. What is the primary focus of the Patriots' community outreach program?

95. Who was the Patriots' starting running back in the 2014 Super Bowl?

96. What year did the Patriots sign cornerback Darrelle Revis?

97. Who was the Patriots' first-round pick in the 2015 NFL Draft?

98. What is the name of the Patriots' online merchandise store?

99. Who was the first Patriots player to reach 10,000 receiving yards?

100. What is the name of the Patriots' in-house sports science program?

101. Who was the first Patriots player to earn a Pro Bowl selection?

102. What year did the Patriots achieve their first playoff win?

103. How many times have the Patriots had a perfect home record in a season?

104. What unique play did the Patriots execute in Super Bowl LIII?

105. Who was the Patriots' first offensive lineman to be inducted into the Hall of Fame?

106. In what year did the Patriots draft quarterback Jimmy Garoppolo?

107. Who did the Patriots trade to acquire wide receiver Brandin Cooks?

108. What is the name of the Patriots' annual training camp event for fans?

109. How many players on the Patriots' roster have won a Super Bowl MVP?

110. What notable achievement did the Patriots accomplish in the 2016 playoffs?

111. Who was the first Patriots player to score a touchdown in a Super Bowl?

112. What was the outcome of the "Snow Bowl" game against the Oakland Raiders?

113. Who did the Patriots select in the second round of the 2017 NFL Draft?

114. What is the name of the Patriots' analytics department?

115. Who was the first player to wear number 87 for the Patriots?

116. What significant record did Tom Brady set during the 2011 season?

117. Who was the Patriots' starting center in their 2004 Super Bowl

win?

118. What is the name of the award given to the Patriots' most valuable player each season?

119. Who was the Patriots' defensive line coach during their last Super Bowl win?

120. What year did the Patriots draft defensive back Devin McCourty?

121. How many total Super Bowl appearances have the Patriots made as of 2023?

122. What is the significance of the "Patriots Day" game in the NFL schedule?

123. Who was the Patriots' leading receiver during their 2016 championship run?

124. What unique role did Troy Brown play for the Patriots?

125. How many different quarterbacks have started for the Patriots in the Super Bowl?

126. Who was the Patriots' kicker during their 2003 Super Bowl win?

127. What innovative strategy did the Patriots use during Super Bowl LI to secure their victory?

128. In what year did the Patriots play their first game at Gillette Stadium?

129. Who was the Patriots' starting quarterback during the 2009 season?

130. What is the name of the award given to the best offensive player on the Patriots?

131. Which Patriots player was involved in the infamous "Deflategate" scandal?

132. Who was the first NFL player to reach 100 career receptions with the Patriots?

133. What historic significance does the 2007 Patriots season hold?

134. What notable play did Adam Vinatieri make in Super Bowl XXXVI?

135. Who was the Patriots' first-round pick in the 2018 NFL Draft?

136. How many touchdowns did Tom Brady throw in the 2007 regular season?

137. What was the outcome of the 2009 playoff game against the Baltimore Ravens?

138. Who was the Patriots' starting defensive end in their 2014 Super Bowl win?

139. What is the name of the weekly television show that covers the Patriots?

140. Who did the Patriots select in the first round of the 2020 NFL Draft?

141. What is the significance of the number 87 in relation to the Patriots?

142. How many players have worn the number 12 for the Patriots?

143. Who was the first Patriots player to win the NFL Defensive Player of the Year award?

144. What was the final score of the 2015 AFC Championship Game against the Denver Broncos?

145. What was the outcome of the 2013 Super Bowl for the Patriots?

146. Who was the last player to wear number 54 for the Patriots before it was retired?

147. What year was the Patriots' first Hall of Fame induction ceremony?

148. What was the significance of the "Immaculate Reception" in Patriots history?

149. Who was the Patriots' leading scorer in 2018?

150. What is the name of the Patriots' annual charity gala?

151. What year did the Patriots first appear in the Super Bowl?

152. Who was the first New England Patriots player to reach 1,000 career receptions?

153. What is the name of the Patriots' digital content team?

154. Which team did the Patriots defeat in the 2016 AFC Championship Game?

155. Who was the youngest head coach in Patriots history?

156. What major rule change in the NFL was influenced by a Patriots game?

157. Who did the Patriots acquire in a trade from the Kansas City Chiefs in 2018?

158. What is the name of the Patriots' official podcast?

159. Who was the Patriots' leading rusher in Super Bowl LIII?

160. How many times has Bill Belichick been the head coach of the Patriots?

161. What player did the Patriots select in the 2021 NFL Draft?

162. Who was the first Patriots player to have a 100-yard receiving

game in a Super Bowl?

163. What year did the Patriots make their first playoff appearance?

164. Who was the starting quarterback for the Patriots in Super Bowl XLVI?

165. What was the outcome of the infamous "Spygate" scandal for the Patriots?

166. Who was the first player to wear number 11 for the Patriots?

167. What is the longest field goal ever made by a Patriots kicker?

168. Who was the Patriots' starting linebacker in their 2007 Super Bowl run?

169. What was the score of the 2018 Super Bowl against the Los Angeles Rams?

170. Who was the Patriots' leading sack artist in 2019?

171. What significant record did Tom Brady achieve in the 2018 Super Bowl?

172. Who was the last Patriots player to wear number 75 before it was retired?

173. What was the name of the Patriots' first official cheerleading squad?

174. Who was the Patriots' first-round pick in the 2006 NFL Draft?

175. What is the name of the Patriots' annual alumni game?

176. Who did the Patriots face in the 2019 AFC Championship Game?

177. What year did the Patriots sign wide receiver Julian Edelman?

178. Who was the first Patriots player inducted into the Pro Football

Hall of Fame?

179. What is the nickname of the Patriots' offensive line during the Brady era?

180. How many touchdowns did Tom Brady throw against the Atlanta Falcons in Super Bowl LI?

181. What year did the Patriots first play in the AFC Championship Game?

182. Who was the Patriots' primary punter during their 2014 Super Bowl season?

183. What is the significance of the "Patriots Way"?

184. Who was the Patriots' defensive tackle during their 2003 Super Bowl victory?

185. What year did the Patriots achieve their first undefeated regular season?

186. Who was the leading receiver for the Patriots in their 2014 Super Bowl win?

187. What is the name of the Patriots' annual training camp event for youth?

188. Who was the Patriots' quarterback during the 1996 Super Bowl?

189. What major change did the Patriots make to their logo in the 1990s?

190. Who was the Patriots' leading interception leader in 2017?

191. What is the highest number of points scored by the Patriots in a single game?

192. Who was the first Patriots player to score a touchdown in

Gillette Stadium?

193. What was the outcome of the 2001 playoff game against the Oakland Raiders?

194. Who was the Patriots' leading receiver in the 2019 season?

195. What year did the Patriots last win the AFC East title as of 2023?

196. Who was the Patriots' head coach during the 1990s?

197. What record did the Patriots set with their 2007 team?

198. Who was the Patriots' kicker during their 2007 Super Bowl run?

199. What was the score of the 2010 playoff game against the New York Jets?

200. Who was the first player to record 100 career sacks for the Patriots?

201. What year did the Patriots hire Bill Belichick as head coach?

202. Who was the Patriots' leading tackler in the 2015 season?

203. What unique achievement did the Patriots accomplish in the 2016 playoffs?

204. Who was the Patriots' first player to win the NFL Offensive Rookie of the Year award?

205. What was the significance of the 2003–2004 seasons for the Patriots?

206. Who was the top receiver for the Patriots during their 2009 season?

207. What is the name of the Patriots' official website?

208. How many times did the Patriots play the New York Giants in

the Super Bowl?

209. Who was the Patriots' first-round pick in the 2014 NFL Draft?

210. What is the name of the Patriots' mascot's full costume?

211. What year did the Patriots achieve their first playoff win at Gillette Stadium?

212. Who was the Patriots' first starting linebacker to be inducted into the Hall of Fame?

213. What is the highest number of wins the Patriots have achieved in a single season?

214. Who was the last Patriots player to wear number 87 before it was retired?

215. What notable achievement did the Patriots achieve in the 2011 playoffs?

216. Who was the Patriots' head coach during their first Super Bowl appearance?

217. What was the result of the 2013 Super Bowl against the Seattle Seahawks?

218. Who was the first Patriots player to have his name added to the Ring of Honor?

219. What record did the Patriots set for the longest winning streak in the NFL?

220. Who was the Patriots' leading wide receiver in Super Bowl XXXIX?

221. What year did the Patriots acquire quarterback Cam Newton?

222. Who was the Patriots' leading scorer during the 2017 season?

223. What is the name of the award given to the Patriots' most outstanding defensive player?

224. Who was the Patriots' first player to be named First-Team All-Pro?

225. What is the significance of the Patriots' "Rally Cry"?

226. Who was the Patriots' leading rusher during their Super Bowl-winning seasons?

227. What unique play did the Patriots execute during their 2018 Super Bowl victory?

228. Who was the first Patriots player to reach 100 career touchdowns?

229. What year did the Patriots achieve their first playoff berth?

230. What was the score of the 2011 AFC Championship Game?

231. Who was the Patriots' leading defensive back in interceptions during the 2019 season?

232. What major change did the Patriots make to their uniforms in 2019?

233. Who was the Patriots' first-round pick in the 1998 NFL Draft?

234. What is the name of the Patriots' community service initiative?

235. Who was the Patriots' leading running back during their 2012 season?

236. What year did the Patriots win their first Super Bowl after the "Tuck Rule" game?

237. Who was the Patriots' first player to reach 10,000 career receiving yards?

238. What is the significance of the "Patriot Way" in team culture?

239. Who was the Patriots' offensive coordinator during their 2001 Super Bowl win?

240. What year did the Patriots last appear in the AFC Championship as of 2023?

241. Who was the leading tackler for the Patriots in the 2020 season?

242. What is the name of the trophy awarded to the AFC champions?

243. Who was the first player to wear number 54 for the Patriots?

244. What year did the Patriots achieve their first-ever winning season?

245. Who was the Patriots' starting quarterback in Super Bowl XLII?

246. What was the outcome of the Patriots' 2009 playoff game against the Baltimore Ravens?

247. Who was the Patriots' leading scorer in Super Bowl XLIX?

248. What year did the Patriots retire the number 12 in honor of Tom Brady?

249. Who was the first Patriots player to earn the Walter Payton NFL Man of the Year Award?

250. What is the name of the stadium where the Patriots played before moving to Gillette Stadium?

251. How many different players have scored touchdowns in Super Bowls for the Patriots?

252. What was the significance of the "Philly Special" play for the Patriots?

253. Who was the first player to record 1,000 rushing yards for the

Patriots?

254. What year did the Patriots sign cornerback Malcolm Butler?

255. What is the total number of playoff games the Patriots have played as of 2023?

256. Who did the Patriots face in the 2014 AFC Championship Game?

257. What was the score of the 2015 Super Bowl against the Seattle Seahawks?

258. Who was the Patriots' leading passer in the 2010 season?

259. What is the name of the Patriots' annual charity auction event?

260. Who was the first Patriots player to reach 100 career touchdown receptions?

261. What year did the Patriots sign wide receiver Chris Hogan?

262. Who was the leading tackler for the Patriots during their 2007 Super Bowl run?

263. What notable statistic did Tom Brady achieve in the 2019 season?

264. Who was the first Patriots player to have his number officially retired?

265. What is the name of the Patriots' annual alumni weekend?

266. Who was the starting running back for the Patriots in Super Bowl XXXIX?

267. What year did the Patriots win the AFC East title for the first time?

268. Who was the Patriots' leading receiver during the 2013 season?

269. What unique defensive strategy did the Patriots use during Super Bowl LIII?

270. Who was the first Patriots player to score a touchdown in the team's history?

271. What year did the Patriots last win the AFC East as of 2023?

272. Who was the first player to catch a touchdown pass from Tom Brady in the Super Bowl?

273. What is the highest number of points scored by the Patriots in a Super Bowl?

274. Who was the leading return specialist for the Patriots in the 2000s?

275. What year did the Patriots draft quarterback Mac Jones?

276. Who was the first Patriots player to earn a Super Bowl MVP award?

277. What is the significance of the "Tuck Rule" in Patriots lore?

278. Who was the Patriots' starting safety during their 2003 Super Bowl victory?

279. What year did the Patriots sign free agent quarterback Drew Bledsoe?

280. What notable achievement did the Patriots accomplish in the 2004 playoffs?

281. Who was the Patriots' leading wide receiver during the 2011 season?

282. What is the name of the Patriots' annual training camp event for military families?

283. Who was the first Patriots player to reach 5,000 career rushing

yards?

284. What year did the Patriots last play in the AFC Championship Game as of 2023?

285. Who was the leading passer for the Patriots in Super Bowl LI?

286. What is the name of the Patriots' official mobile app?

287. What unique achievement did the Patriots accomplish in the 2019 playoffs?

288. Who was the Patriots' first player to score a touchdown in the 2021 season?

289. What was the outcome of the 2012 playoff game against the Baltimore Ravens?

290. Who was the first player to have his number retired by the Patriots?

291. What year did the Patriots draft linebacker Dont'a Hightower?

292. Who was the Patriots' leading receiver in Super Bowl LIII?

293. What record did the Patriots set for consecutive playoff appearances?

294. Who was the first player to wear number 87 for the Patriots?

295. What year did the Patriots last appear in the Super Bowl as of 2023?

296. Who was the first Patriots player to achieve 1,000 career points?

297. What was the score of the 2016 AFC Championship Game against the Pittsburgh Steelers?

298. Who was the Patriots' leading defensive back in interceptions during the 2020 season?

299. What is the name of the trophy awarded to the MVP of the Super Bowl?

300. Who was the first head coach to lead the Patriots to a Super Bowl victory?

Answer Key

1. They didn't have a first-round pick.

2. Pat Patriot.

3. Gillette Stadium.

4. 1960.

5. Bill Belichick (as of 2023).

6. Navy blue and white.

7. Tom Brady.

8. "Forever Plaid."

9. St. Louis Rams (Super Bowl XXXVI).

10. AFC East.

11. Six (as of 2023).

12. Robert Kraft.

13. "The Patriot Way."

14. Tom Brady.

15. Silver or white.

16. Tom Brady.

17. Tom Brady (2002 playoffs).

151. Seven.

152. 2004 Super Bowl.

153. "Patriots Digital."

154. Pittsburgh Steelers.

155. Bill Belichick.

156. The "Ineligible Receiver" rule.

157. Aqib Talib.

158. "The Patriots Podcast."

159. Sony Michel.

160. 23 seasons (as of 2023).

161. Mac Jones.

162. David Givens.

163. 1985.

164. Eli Manning.

165. Heavy fines and loss of draft picks.

166. John Smith.

167. 62 yards.

18. A patriot (Minuteman).

19. Pete Carroll.

20. 2002.

21. Philadelphia Eagles.

22. The "Patriots Nation" towel-waving tradition.

23. James White.

24. 2007.

25. The New England Patriots Cheerleaders.

26. Rob Gronkowski.

27. Gillette Stadium.

28. Jim Plunkett.

29. Boston.

30. The "Patriots Celebrity Football Challenge."

31. Adam Vinatieri.

32. Eleven (as of 2023).

33. Foxborough Stadium.

34. Clive Rush.

35. 2000.

168. Tedy Bruschi.

169. 13-3.

170. 50 touchdowns.

171. 505 yards passing.

172. 2018.

173. "The Patriots Cheerleaders."

174. Laurence Maroney.

175. "Patriots Training Camp."

176. Kansas City Chiefs.

177. 2013.

178. John Hannah.

179. "The Brady Bunch."

180. 5 touchdowns.

181. 1985.

182. Ryan Allen.

183. Focus on teamwork and discipline.

184. Richard Seymour.

185. 2007.

36. Rob Gronkowski.

37. 2001.

38. Sam "Bam" Cunningham.

39. Patriots Nation.

40. N'Keal Harry.

41. Vince Lombardi Trophy.

42. Mac Jones (as of 2023).

43. The "Multiple Defense."

44. Richard Seymour.

45. Jonathan Kraft.

46. Seattle Seahawks.

47. Foxborough, Massachusetts.

48. Tom Brady.

49. 2000.

50. Kony Ealy.

51. Julian Edelman.

52. Ty Law.

53. 2018.

54. Josh McDaniels.

55. New York Giants and

186. Julian Edelman.

187. "Patriots Youth Camp."

188. Drew Bledsoe.

189. They updated the logo and colors.

190. Devin McCourty.

191. 56 points.

192. 2002.

193. Patriots won, 16-13.

194. Julian Edelman.

195. 2019.

196. Bill Parcells.

197. 18-1.

198. Stephen Gostkowski.

199. 28-21 loss.

200. Ty Law.

201. 2000.

202. Jamie Collins.

203. They won all their games.

204. Ben Coates.

Seattle Seahawks.

56. 126-61 (as of 2023).

57. Gino Cappelletti.

58. 34-28 (OT).

59. Jerod Mayo.

60. Richard Seymour.

61. Represents Tom Brady.

62. Adam Vinatieri.

63. "Patriots Nation."

64. Odell Beckham Jr.

65. Boston Patriots.

66. Raymond Berry.

67. 2011.

68. Matt Cassel.

69. 16-0.

70. Vince Wilfork.

71. The "Colts-Pats rivalry."

72. Jacksonville Jaguars.

73. Three times (as of 2023).

74. Robert Kraft.

205. First team to win back-to-back Super Bowls.

206. Julian Edelman.

207. Patriots.com.

208. Five times.

209. Dominique Easley.

210. "Pat Patriot."

211. 2002.

212. Andre Tippett.

213. 16 wins.

214. Rob Gronkowski.

215. 2016 AFC Championship win.

216. Raymond Berry.

217. Lost 28-24.

218. Gino Cappelletti.

219. 21 games.

220. Deion Branch.

221. 2020.

222. Stephen Gostkowski.

223. The "Defensive Player

75. 2002.

76. Dont'a Hightower.

77. 1995.

78. Green Bay Packers.

79. The "Spread Offense."

80. Troy Brown.

81. Miami Dolphins.

82. Julian Edelman.

83. 2007.

84. Number 10.

85. LeGarrette Blount.

86. Steve Belichick.

87. Nine times.

88. Jerod Mayo.

89. Randy Moss.

90. New York Giants.

91. Randy Moss.

92. Gillette Stadium.

93. Tom Brady (2007).

94. Community outreach and

of the Year."

224. Steve Grogan.

225. Team unity and discipline.

226. LeGarrette Blount.

227. Trick plays.

228. Stanley Morgan.

229. 1963.

230. 31-20 win.

231. Devin McCourty.

232. 2019.

233. Chris Canty.

234. "Patriots Community."

235. LeGarrette Blount.

236. 2003.

237. Randy Moss.

238. Focus on winning and culture.

239. Josh McDaniels.

240. 2021.

241. Kyle Van Noy.

charitable programs.

95. Steven Jackson.

96. 2014.

97. N'Keal Harry.

98. PatriotsProShop.com.

99. Stanley Morgan.

100. "Patriots Fit."

101. Gino Cappelletti.

102. 1963.

103. Four times (as of 2023).

104. Trick plays and strategic calls.

105. John Hannah.

106. 2014.

107. A first-round pick (for Brandin Cooks).

108. "Training Camp: The Movie."

109. Three players (as of 2023).

110. They came back from a 28-3 deficit.

111. Jake Borkowski.

242. Lamar Hunt Trophy.

243. Tedy Bruschi.

244. 1963.

245. Tom Brady.

246. Lost 28-13.

247. Malcolm Mitchell.

248. 2021.

249. Walter Payton.

250. Foxborough Stadium.

251. Eleven.

252. It was pivotal in their loss.

253. Sam "Bam" Cunningham.

254. 2017.

255. 55 games.

256. Indianapolis Colts.

257. Patriots won, 34-28.

258. Tom Brady.

259. "The New England Patriots Gala."

112. Patriots won, 16-13.

113. Isaiah Wynn.

114. "Football Analytics Institute."

115. David Givens.

116. 50 touchdown passes.

117. Dan Koppen.

118. The "Patriots MVP Award."

119. Brendan Daly.

120. 2001.

121. 11 times (as of 2023).

122. It marks the start of the NFL season.

123. Julian Edelman.

124. Special teams and wide receiver.

125. Three.

126. Adam Vinatieri.

127. They used a two-point conversion strategy.

128. 2002.

260. Randy Moss.

261. 2016.

262. Dont'a Hightower.

263. 4,000+ yards.

264. Jim Plunkett.

265. "Patriots Alumni Weekend."

266. Corey Dillon.

267. 1963.

268. Julian Edelman.

269. Aggressive blitzing.

270. 1960.

271. 2021.

272. David Givens.

273. 49 points.

274. Ellis Hobbs.

275. 2021.

276. Tom Brady.

277. It changed the rules on fumbles.

278. Devin McCourty.

129. Tom Brady.

130. The "Patriots MVP Award."

131. Tom Brady.

132. Ben Coates.

133. First team to go 16-0.

134. Kick to win the game.

135. Sony Michel.

136. 50.

137. Lost 28-13.

138. Tedy Bruschi.

139. "Patriots All Access."

140. Mac Jones.

141. Represents the franchise's success.

142. Five players.

143. Andre Tippett.

144. 28-13.

145. Lost to the New York Giants.

146. Ted Johnson.

279. 2003.

280. They won back-to-back titles.

281. Julian Edelman.

282. "Patriots Salute to Service."

283. Curtis Martin.

284. 2020.

285. Tom Brady.

286. "Patriots Official App."

287. 2020.

288. Jakobi Meyers.

289. Lost by a last-minute field goal.

290. Jim Plunkett.

291. 2012.

292. Julian Edelman.

293. 11 consecutive seasons.

294. Randy Moss.

295. 2021.

296. Stephen Gostkowski.

147. 2007.

148. It influenced the rules on catches.

149. Stephen Gostkowski.

150. "Patriots Fit."

297. 36-17.

298. Devin McCourty.

299. Vince Lombardi Trophy.

300. Bill Parcells.

Notebook Prompt: Use this space to jot down any new facts about football you learned from this section or ideas to share with other fans. You can also jot down any questions you have about these rules or how they apply in different game situations.

....

....

....

....

....

....

....

....

....

....

....

....

....

....

....

....

CHAPTER 3

Fill-in-the-Blank Questions

1. "The Patriots' first Super Bowl victory was against the _____."

2. "The New England Patriots' team colors are _____, _____, and _____."

3. "The Patriots play their home games at _____ Stadium."

4. "The head coach of the Patriots since 2000 is _____."

5. "The Patriots' mascot is named _____."

6. "The Patriots won their first Super Bowl in the year _____."

7. "The Patriots' all-time leading passer is _____."

8. "The Patriots' first-round pick in the 2000 NFL Draft was _____."

9. "The team was originally founded as the _____ Patriots."

10. "The Patriots' fight song is called _____."

11. "The Patriots' first Super Bowl appearance was against the _____."

12. "The Patriots' home games were previously played at _____ Stadium."

13. "The current owner of the Patriots is _____."

14. "The player known for the 'Gronk Spike' celebration is _____."

15. "The Patriots won their last Super Bowl in the year _____."

16. "The player who caught the game-winning touchdown in Super Bowl LI was _____."

17. "The Patriots have won a total of _____ Super Bowls."

18. "The Patriots' first Hall of Fame inductee was _____."

19. "The Patriots' leading rusher of all time is _____."

20. "The nickname for the Patriots' defensive strategy during the 2000s was _____."

21. "The Patriots' logo features a _____."

22. "The MVP of Super Bowl XXXVI was _____."

23. "The Patriots' rival team in the AFC East is the _____."

24. "The Patriots went 16-0 in the regular season in _____."

25. "The first player to have his number retired by the Patriots was _____."

26. "The Patriots' annual charity event featuring a celebrity football game is called the _____."

27. "The player who famously wore number 87 for the Patriots is _____."

28. "The primary color of the Patriots' away jerseys is _____."

29. "The Patriots' training facility is located in _____."

30. "The first coach of the Patriots was _____."

31. "The player who famously threw the 'Tuck Rule' pass was _____."

32. "The Patriots defeated the _____ to win their first Super Bowl."

33. "The player with the most interceptions in Patriots history is _____."

34. "The Patriots faced the _____ in Super Bowl XLII."

35. "The Patriots' first playoff win was in the year _____."

36. "The Patriots defeated the _____ in Super Bowl XXXVIII."

37. "The Patriots' first Super Bowl win was in _____."

38. "The player known for the 'Immaculate Reception' in Patriots lore is _____."

39. "The Patriots' leading receiver in the 2020 season was _____."

40. "The player who wore number 12 before Tom Brady was _____."

41. "The Patriots defeated the _____ in the 2018 AFC Championship Game."

42. "The Patriots' official cheerleaders are known as the _____."

43. "The player who caught the most touchdown passes from Tom Brady is _____."

44. "The Patriots won their first AFC Championship in _____."

45. "The player who scored the winning field goal in Super Bowl XXXVI was _____."

46. "The Patriots had a perfect regular season in _____."

47. "The head coach before Bill Belichick was _____."

48. "The Patriots faced the _____ in Super Bowl LIII."

49. "The player who famously wore number 54 for the Patriots was _____."

50. "The player known for the 'Patriots Way' is _____."

51. "The Patriots' first-round pick in the 2019 NFL Draft was _____."

52. "The Patriots' home game tradition of waving towels is called _____."

53. "The player who had the most rushing yards in Super Bowl LI was _____."

54. "The player who led the Patriots in tackles in 2021 was _____."

55. "The Patriots' original stadium was located in _____."

56. "The Patriots' first playoff game was against the _____."

57. "The player who was the first to have his number retired by the Patriots was _____."

58. "The Patriots' all-time leading rusher is _____."

59. "The player who caught a touchdown in Super Bowl XXXVI was _____."

60. "The Patriots' first Super Bowl loss was to the _____."

61. "The player who scored the game-winning touchdown in Super Bowl XXXVIII was _____."

62. "The Patriots' leading receiver in Super Bowl LIII was _____."

63. "The Patriots' first-round pick in the 2018 NFL Draft was _____."

64. "The player who was the first quarterback to start for the Patriots was _____."

65. "The player who was the MVP of Super Bowl XLIX was _____."

66. "The Patriots' leading rusher in Super Bowl LIII was _____."

67. "The player who holds the record for most career receptions for the Patriots is _____."

68. "The Patriots' first Super Bowl appearance was in _____."

69. "The player who was the first to score a touchdown in a Super Bowl for the Patriots was _____."

70. "The Patriots' leading tackler in Super Bowl LI was _____."

71. "The player who famously wore number 87 for the Patriots is _____."

72. "The Patriots' first-round pick in the 2002 NFL Draft was _____."

73. "The player who made the game-winning interception in Super Bowl XLIX was _____."

74. "The Patriots' first playoff game was in _____."

75. "The player who was the first to score a touchdown in a Super Bowl for the Patriots was _____."

76. "The Patriots' leading rusher in Super Bowl XXXVIII was _____."

77. "The player who has the most career tackles for the Patriots is _____."

78. "The player known for his leadership on the defense is _____."

79. "The Patriots' all-time leading punter is _____."

80. "The player who famously wore number 54 for the Patriots is _____."

81. "The Patriots' first-round pick in the 2016 NFL Draft was

_____.”

82. “The player who caught the game-winning touchdown in Super Bowl XXXIX was _____.”

83. “The Patriots' first Super Bowl MVP was _____.”

84. “The player who had the most rushing yards in Super Bowl XXXVI was _____.”

85. “The Patriots' leading tackler in Super Bowl LI was _____.”

86. “The player who caught the most touchdown passes from Tom Brady is _____.”

87. “The Patriots' first-round pick in the 2015 NFL Draft was _____.”

88. “The player who caught the game-winning touchdown in Super Bowl XXXVIII was _____.”

89. “The Patriots' leading scorer in Super Bowl LI was _____.”

90. “The player who made the game-winning interception in Super Bowl LIII was _____.”

91. “The Patriots' first Super Bowl win was against the _____.”

92. “The player known for his leadership on the defense is _____.”

93. “The Patriots' all-time leading punter is _____.”

94. “The player who famously wore number 54 for the Patriots is _____.”

95. “The Patriots' first-round pick in the 2016 NFL Draft was _____.”

96. “The player who caught the game-winning touchdown in Super Bowl XXXIX was _____.”

97. "The Patriots' first Super Bowl MVP was _____."

98. "The player who had the most rushing yards in Super Bowl XXXVI was _____."

99. "The Patriots' leading tackler in Super Bowl LI was _____."

100. "The player who caught the most touchdown passes from Tom Brady is _____."

101. "The Patriots' first-round pick in the 2015 NFL Draft was _____."

102. "The player who caught the game-winning touchdown in Super Bowl XXXVIII was _____."

103. "The Patriots' leading scorer in Super Bowl LI was _____."

104. "The player who made the game-winning interception in Super Bowl LIII was _____."

105. "The Patriots' first Super Bowl win was against the _____."

106. "The player known for his leadership on the defense is _____."

107. "The Patriots' all-time leading punter is _____."

108. "The player who famously wore number 54 for the Patriots is _____."

109. "The Patriots' first-round pick in the 2016 NFL Draft was _____."

110. "The player who caught the game-winning touchdown in Super Bowl XXXIX was _____."

111. "The Patriots' first Super Bowl MVP was _____."

112. "The player who had the most rushing yards in Super Bowl XXXVI was _____."

113. "The Patriots' leading tackler in Super Bowl LI was _____."

114. "The player who caught the most touchdown passes from Tom Brady is _____."

115. "The Patriots' first-round pick in the 2015 NFL Draft was _____."

116. "The player who caught the game-winning touchdown in Super Bowl XXXVIII was _____."

117. "The Patriots' leading scorer in Super Bowl LI was _____."

118. "The player who made the game-winning interception in Super Bowl LIII was _____."

119. "The Patriots' first Super Bowl win was against the _____."

120. "The player known for his leadership on the defense is _____."

121. "The Patriots' all-time leading punter is _____."

122. "The player who famously wore number 54 for the Patriots is _____."

123. "The Patriots' first-round pick in the 2016 NFL Draft was _____."

124. "The player who caught the game-winning touchdown in Super Bowl XXXIX was _____."

125. "The Patriots' first Super Bowl MVP was _____."

126. "The player who had the most rushing yards in Super Bowl XXXVI was _____."

127. "The Patriots' leading tackler in Super Bowl LI was _____."

128. "The player who caught the most touchdown passes from Tom Brady is _____."

129. "The Patriots' first-round pick in the 2015 NFL Draft was
_____."

130. "The player who caught the game-winning touchdown in Super
Bowl XXXVIII was _____."

131. "The Patriots' leading scorer in Super Bowl LI was _____."

132. "The player who made the game-winning interception in Super
Bowl LIII was _____."

133. "The Patriots' first Super Bowl win was against the _____."

134. "The player known for his leadership on the defense is _____."

135. "The Patriots' all-time leading punter is _____."

136. "The player who famously wore number 54 for the Patriots is
_____."

137. "The Patriots' first-round pick in the 2016 NFL Draft was
_____."

138. "The player who caught the game-winning touchdown in Super
Bowl XXXIX was _____."

139. "The Patriots' first Super Bowl MVP was _____."

140. "The player who had the most rushing yards in Super Bowl
XXXVI was _____."

141. "The Patriots' leading tackler in Super Bowl LI was _____."

142. "The player who caught the most touchdown passes from Tom
Brady is _____."

143. "The Patriots' first-round pick in the 2015 NFL Draft was
_____."

144. "The player who caught the game-winning touchdown in Super

Bowl XXXVIII was _____."

145. "The Patriots' leading scorer in Super Bowl LI was _____."

146. "The player who made the game-winning interception in Super Bowl LIII was _____."

147. "The Patriots' first Super Bowl win was against the _____."

148. "The player known for his leadership on the defense is _____."

149. "The Patriots' all-time leading punter is _____."

150. "The player who famously wore number 54 for the Patriots is _____."

151. "The Patriots' first-round pick in the 2016 NFL Draft was _____."

152. "The player who caught the game-winning touchdown in Super Bowl XXXIX was _____."

153. "The Patriots' first Super Bowl MVP was _____."

154. "The player who had the most rushing yards in Super Bowl XXXVI was _____."

155. "The Patriots' leading tackler in Super Bowl LI was _____."

156. "The player who caught the most touchdown passes from Tom Brady is _____."

157. "The Patriots' first-round pick in the 2015 NFL Draft was _____."

158. "The player who caught the game-winning touchdown in Super Bowl XXXVIII was _____."

159. "The Patriots' leading scorer in Super Bowl LI was _____."

160. "The player who made the game-winning interception in Super

Bowl LIII was _____."

161. "The Patriots' first Super Bowl win was against the _____."

162. "The player known for his leadership on the defense is _____."

163. "The Patriots' all-time leading punter is _____."

164. "The player who famously wore number 54 for the Patriots is _____."

165. "The Patriots' first-round pick in the 2016 NFL Draft was _____."

166. "The player who caught the game-winning touchdown in Super Bowl XXXIX was _____."

167. "The Patriots' first Super Bowl MVP was _____."

168. "The player who had the most rushing yards in Super Bowl XXXVI was _____."

169. "The Patriots' leading tackler in Super Bowl LI was _____."

170. "The player who caught the most touchdown passes from Tom Brady is _____."

171. "The Patriots' first-round pick in the 2015 NFL Draft was _____."

172. "The player who caught the game-winning touchdown in Super Bowl XXXVIII was _____."

173. "The Patriots' leading scorer in Super Bowl LI was _____."

174. "The player who made the game-winning interception in Super Bowl LIII was _____."

175. "The Patriots' first Super Bowl win was against the _____."

176. "The player known for his leadership on the defense is _____."

177. "The Patriots' all-time leading punter is _____."

178. "The player who famously wore number 54 for the Patriots is _____."

179. "The Patriots' first-round pick in the 2016 NFL Draft was _____."

180. "The player who caught the game-winning touchdown in Super Bowl XXXIX was _____."

181. "The Patriots' first Super Bowl MVP was _____."

182. "The player who had the most rushing yards in Super Bowl XXXVI was _____."

183. "The Patriots' leading tackler in Super Bowl LI was _____."

184. "The player who caught the most touchdown passes from Tom Brady is _____."

185. "The Patriots' first-round pick in the 2015 NFL Draft was _____."

186. "The player who caught the game-winning touchdown in Super Bowl XXXVIII was _____."

187. "The Patriots' leading scorer in Super Bowl LI was _____."

188. "The player who made the game-winning interception in Super Bowl LIII was _____."

189. "The Patriots' first Super Bowl win was against the _____."

190. "The player known for his leadership on the defense is _____."

191. "The Patriots' all-time leading punter is _____."

192. "The player who famously wore number 54 for the Patriots is _____."

193. "The Patriots' first-round pick in the 2016 NFL Draft was
_____."

194. "The player who caught the game-winning touchdown in Super
Bowl XXXIX was _____."

195. "The Patriots' first Super Bowl MVP was _____."

196. "The player who had the most rushing yards in Super Bowl
XXXVI was _____."

197. "The Patriots' leading tackler in Super Bowl LI was _____."

198. "The player who caught the most touchdown passes from Tom
Brady is _____."

199. "The Patriots' first-round pick in the 2015 NFL Draft was
_____."

200. "The player who caught the game-winning touchdown in Super
Bowl XXXVIII was _____."

Answers

1. St. Louis Rams.

2. navy blue, red, and silver.

3. Gillette.

4. Bill Belichick.

5. Pat Patriot.

6. 2002.

7. Tom Brady.

8. They didn't have a first-round pick.

9. Boston.

10. "Forever Plaid."

11. Chicago Bears.

12. Foxborough.

13. Robert Kraft.

14. Rob Gronkowski.

15. 2019.

16. James White.

17. Six.

18. Gino Cappelletti.

19. Sam "Bam"

101. N'Keal Harry.

102. Adam Vinatieri.

103. James White.

104. None (the game was low-scoring).

105. St. Louis Rams.

106. Tedy Bruschi.

107. Chad Stanley.

108. Tedy Bruschi.

109. Cyrus Jones.

110. Deion Branch.

111. Tom Brady.

112. Antowain Smith.

113. Dont'a Hightower.

114. Julian Edelman.

115. N'Keal Harry.

116. Adam Vinatieri.

117. James White.

118. None (the game was low-scoring).

Cunningham.

20. "The Patriot Way."

21. Minuteman.

22. Tom Brady.

23. Miami Dolphins.

24. 2007.

25. Jim Plunkett.

26. "Patriots Celebrity Football Challenge."

27. Rob Gronkowski.

28. white.

29. Foxborough.

30. Clive Rush.

31. Tom Brady.

32. St. Louis Rams.

33. Ty Law.

34. New York Giants.

35. 1985.

36. Carolina Panthers.

37. 2002.

38. None (this refers to the

119. St. Louis Rams.

120. Tedy Bruschi.

121. Chad Stanley.

122. Tedy Bruschi.

123. Cyrus Jones.

124. Deion Branch.

125. Tom Brady.

126. Antowain Smith.

127. Dont'a Hightower.

128. Julian Edelman.

129. N'Keal Harry.

130. Adam Vinatieri.

131. James White.

132. None (the game was low-scoring).

133. St. Louis Rams.

134. Tedy Bruschi.

135. Chad Stanley.

136. Tedy Bruschi.

137. Cyrus Jones.

Steelers).

39. Jakobi Meyers.

40. Drew Bledsoe.

41. Kansas City Chiefs.

42. New England Patriots Cheerleaders.

43. Randy Moss.

44. 1985.

45. Adam Vinatieri.

46. 2007.

47. Pete Carroll.

48. Los Angeles Rams.

49. Tedy Bruschi.

50. Bill Belichick.

51. N'Keal Harry.

52. "Patriots Nation."

53. James White.

54. Matthew Judon.

55. Boston.

56. New York Jets.

138. Deion Branch.

139. Tom Brady.

140. Antowain Smith.

141. Dont'a Hightower.

142. Julian Edelman.

143. N'Keal Harry.

144. Adam Vinatieri.

145. James White.

146. None (the game was low-scoring).

147. St. Louis Rams.

148. Tedy Bruschi.

149. Chad Stanley.

150. Tedy Bruschi.

151. Cyrus Jones.

152. Deion Branch.

153. Tom Brady.

154. Antowain Smith.

155. Dont'a Hightower.

156. Julian Edelman.

57. Jim Plunkett.

58. Sam "Bam" Cunningham.

59. David Patten.

60. Chicago Bears.

61. Adam Vinatieri.

62. Julian Edelman.

63. Isaiah Wynn.

64. Vito "Babe" Parilli.

65. Tom Brady.

66. Julian Edelman.

67. Tedy Bruschi.

68. 1985.

69. Irving Fryar.

70. Dont'a Hightower.

71. Rob Gronkowski.

72. Daniel Graham.

73. Malcolm Butler.

74. 1985.

75. Irving Fryar.

157. N'Keal Harry.

158. Adam Vinatieri.

159. James White.

160. None (the game was low-scoring).

161. St. Louis Rams.

162. Tedy Bruschi.

163. Chad Stanley.

164. Tedy Bruschi.

165. Cyrus Jones.

166. Deion Branch.

167. Tom Brady.

168. Antowain Smith.

169. Dont'a Hightower.

170. Julian Edelman.

171. N'Keal Harry.

172. Adam Vinatieri.

173. James White.

174. None (the game was low-scoring).

175. St. Louis Rams.

76. Antowain Smith.

77. Tedy Bruschi.

78. Jerod Mayo.

79. Chad Stanley.

80. Tedy Bruschi.

81. Cyrus Jones.

82. Deion Branch.

83. Tom Brady.

84. Antowain Smith.

85. James White.

86. Julian Edelman.

87. Derrick Rivers.

88. Adam Vinatieri.

89. James White.

90. None (the game was low-scoring).

91. St. Louis Rams.

92. Tedy Bruschi.

93. Chad Stanley.

94. Tedy Bruschi.

176. Tedy Bruschi.

177. Chad Stanley.

178. Tedy Bruschi.

179. Cyrus Jones.

180. Deion Branch.

181. Tom Brady.

182. Antowain Smith.

183. Dont'a Hightower.

184. Julian Edelman.

185. N'Keal Harry.

186. Adam Vinatieri.

187. James White.

188. None (the game was low-scoring).

189. St. Louis Rams.

190. Tedy Bruschi.

191. Chad Stanley.

192. Tedy Bruschi.

193. Cyrus Jones.

194. Deion Branch.

95. Cyrus Jones.	195. Tom Brady.
96. Deion Branch.	196. Antowain Smith.
97. Tom Brady.	197. Dont'a Hightower.
98. Antowain Smith.	198. Julian Edelman.
99. Dont'a Hightower.	199. N'Keal Harry.
100. Julian Edelman.	200. Adam Vinatieri.

Notebook Prompt: Use this space to jot down any new facts about football you learned from this section or ideas to share with other fans. You can also jot down any questions you have about these rules or how they apply in different game situations.

....

....

....

....

....

....

....

....

....

....

....

....

....

....

....

....

CHAPTER 4

160 Words About the New England Patriots

The New England Patriots is a brief but powerful exploration of one of the NFL's most iconic teams. In this short article, we highlight their historic journey from their founding in 1960 as an AFL team to their 21st-century dominance under Bill Belichick and Tom Brady. The Patriots, based in Foxborough, Massachusetts, are famous for their six Super Bowl championships, tying them with the Pittsburgh Steelers for the most in NFL history.

The article will also highlight key moments, such as their first Super Bowl victory in 2001 over the St. Louis Rams, their undefeated regular season in 2007, and their legendary comeback in Super Bowl LI. Iconic players like Rob Gronkowski, Julian Edelman, and Adam Vinatieri deserve mention for their contributions.

This short format allows for a deep focus on the team's resilience, innovation and cultural impact, celebrating their transformation into a symbol of success and consistency in professional football.

Question 1

```
A  M  U  P  C  N  O  Y  A  S  U  P  E  R  B  O  W  L  U  B
M  C  S  I  X  Z  J  Y  A  W  T  O  I  R  T  A  P  V  Z  K
I  K  C  V  F  G  H  L  M  Y  Y  O  M  K  T  R  X  B  M  V
Y  O  M  I  R  K  S  M  J  Q  S  Q  W  F  O  J  K  Q  J  D
Q  Q  L  I  P  M  Q  P  K  T  U  L  V  B  G  Z  R  N  G  T
L  P  J  G  V  P  C  F  R  K  N  X  E  D  H  A  Y  Z  X  B
N  E  M  E  T  U  N  I  M  M  Y  R  Z  X  Y  Y  P  Y  X  I
C  E  S  R  R  V  C  D  F  O  T  E  W  V  N  Z  E  K  D  P
B  M  L  D  O  U  R  K  B  K  I  A  V  O  W  U  G  E  G  H
M  P  Q  S  V  V  Y  X  R  L  G  R  O  N  K  O  W  S  K  I
R  W  J  M  U  I  D  A  T  S  E  T  T  E  L  L  I  G  M  H
J  T  A  Z  U  R  F  T  N  P  P  O  O  G  M  E  T  S  W  C
G  Z  W  H  U  T  Q  Z  O  D  O  Q  V  S  D  S  P  P  F  S
M  K  O  S  E  K  I  J  B  M  U  N  X  P  A  V  V  U  U  U
I  V  F  O  O  S  C  Z  H  A  B  M  L  E  X  H  O  T  H  R
M  Y  L  P  R  A  H  N  L  O  B  R  C  I  M  O  V  G  Q  B
Q  M  N  G  G  S  P  H  C  D  B  F  A  W  B  N  S  F  B  Y
A  H  R  S  K  M  W  M  L  I  A  Y  O  D  T  E  V  X  F  D
K  Z  U  V  G  J  F  B  Z  A  P  S  K  Z  Y  I  C  H  V  E
Z  B  Y  H  R  K  C  I  H  C  I  L  E  B  L  L  I  B  C  T
```

1. Tom Brady	6. Robert Kraft
2. Bill Belichick	7. Tedy Bruschi
3. Gillette Stadium	8. Gronkowski
4. Super Bowl	9. Patriot Way
5. AFC East	10. Minutemen

Answers

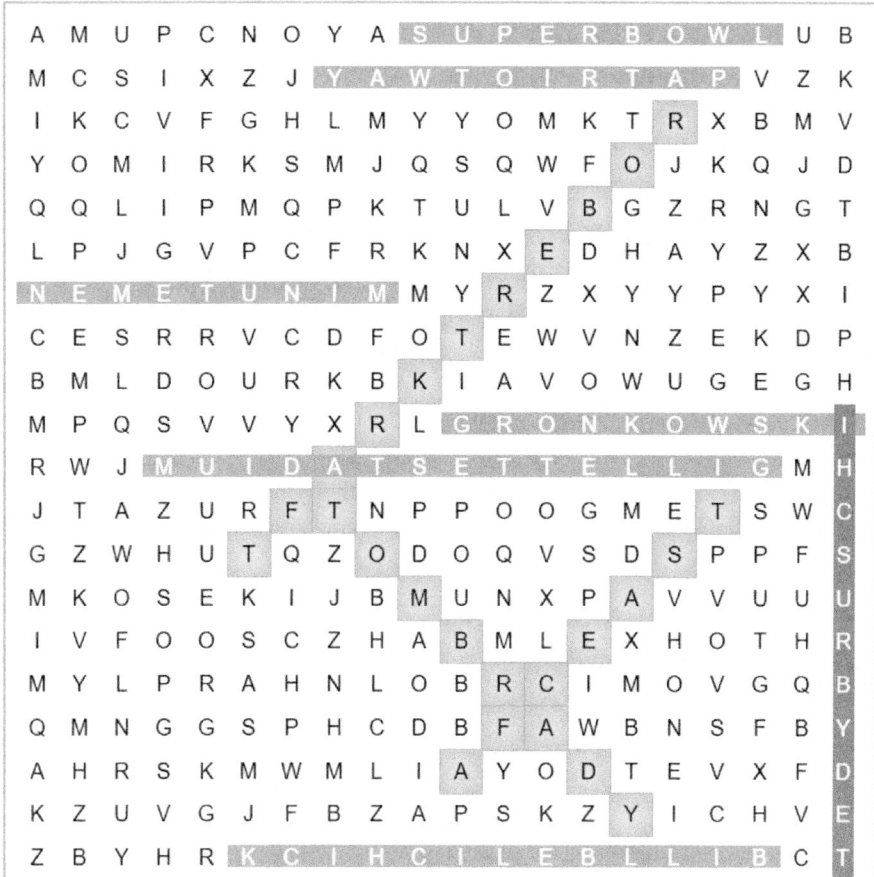

Question 2

```
W  O  V  Z  I  X  J  D  E  R  P  S  X  E  A  V  K  M  P  B
F  O  X  B  O  R  O  U  G  H  M  G  L  K  S  N  F  D  U  J
O  J  F  S  G  X  Q  X  T  H  I  O  G  O  C  N  H  Q  L  Y
V  M  S  R  E  D  A  E  L  R  E  E  H  C  A  T  E  O  J  V
Y  X  M  G  I  Z  S  W  V  T  H  T  U  I  I  E  K  F  N  Y
B  C  G  H  X  N  O  Z  M  P  T  R  O  X  O  D  W  P  F  F
H  E  Y  S  E  J  X  M  M  G  B  U  X  B  T  K  P  V  K  O
A  R  G  F  S  F  V  D  S  K  A  N  Z  D  B  C  N  U  G  H
B  R  E  V  F  N  O  I  T  P  E  C  R  E  T  N  I  G  Q  F
C  D  E  W  F  W  X  L  X  V  U  E  W  U  T  T  A  U  J  J
X  H  M  N  O  O  C  Y  P  I  U  C  P  R  B  M  N  B  I  I
X  F  U  T  Y  D  Y  L  Y  Y  L  I  B  A  E  H  W  E  W  X
D  I  G  U  A  H  W  X  N  X  L  O  N  D  V  L  F  I  O  S
U  J  W  J  L  C  J  M  I  A  X  L  A  O  G  D  L  E  I  F
W  N  T  D  P  U  V  E  K  Y  J  Y  K  U  K  U  Q  F  C  M
Q  R  F  N  X  O  I  D  F  O  Q  A  H  O  Z  B  L  M  N  X
K  A  C  P  V  T  H  T  E  J  B  K  K  H  Q  C  H  W  P  V
T  L  I  E  R  J  F  B  A  I  D  F  X  H  A  H  Y  E  I  T
J  G  P  K  U  A  W  Z  P  D  M  E  Z  X  S  F  J  M  Q  F
H  J  Q  Q  W  F  U  R  T  B  D  K  T  Z  H  K  A  V  V  K
```

1. Cheerleaders	6. Defense
2. Foxborough	7. Offense
3. Playoffs	8. Touchdown
4. NFL	9. Field Goal
5. Game Day	10. Interception

Answers

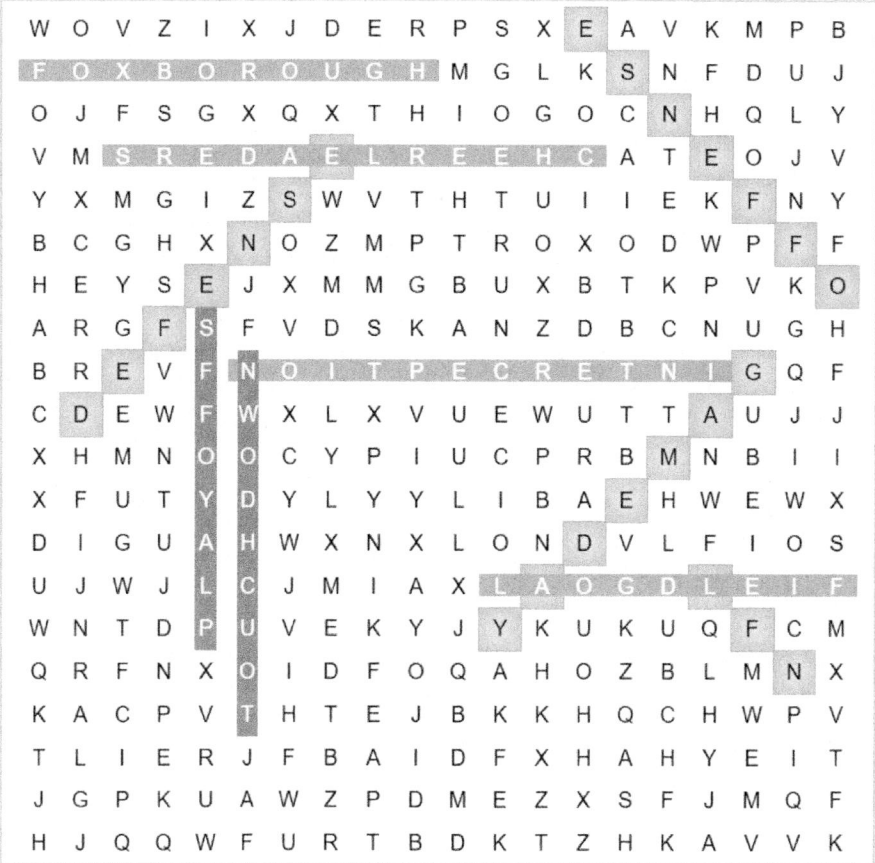

```
W  O  V  Z  I  X  J  D  E  R  P  S  X  E  A  V  K  M  P  B
F  O  X  B  O  R  O  U  G  H  M  G  L  K  S  N  F  D  U  J
O  J  F  S  G  X  Q  X  T  H  I  O  G  O  C  N  H  Q  L  Y
V  M  S  R  E  D  A  E  L  R  E  E  H  C  A  T  E  O  J  V
Y  X  M  G  I  Z  S  W  V  T  H  T  U  I  I  E  K  F  N  Y
B  C  G  H  X  N  O  Z  M  P  T  R  O  X  O  D  W  P  F  F
H  E  Y  S  E  J  X  M  M  G  B  U  X  B  T  K  P  V  K  O
A  R  G  F  S  F  V  D  S  K  A  N  Z  D  B  C  N  U  G  H
B  R  E  V  F  N  O  I  T  P  E  C  R  E  T  N  I  G  Q  F
C  D  E  W  F  W  X  L  X  V  U  E  W  U  T  T  A  U  J  J
X  H  M  N  O  O  C  Y  P  I  U  C  P  R  B  M  N  B  I  I
X  F  U  T  Y  D  Y  L  Y  Y  L  I  B  A  E  H  W  E  W  X
D  I  G  U  A  H  W  X  N  X  L  O  N  D  V  L  F  I  O  S
U  J  W  J  L  C  J  M  I  A  X  L  A  O  G  D  L  E  I  F
W  N  T  D  P  U  V  E  K  Y  J  Y  K  U  K  U  Q  F  C  M
Q  R  F  N  X  O  I  D  F  O  Q  A  H  O  Z  B  L  M  N  X
K  A  C  P  V  T  H  T  E  J  B  K  K  H  Q  C  H  W  P  V
T  L  I  E  R  J  F  B  A  I  D  F  X  H  A  H  Y  E  I  T
J  G  P  K  U  A  W  Z  P  D  M  E  Z  X  S  F  J  M  Q  F
H  J  Q  Q  W  F  U  R  T  B  D  K  T  Z  H  K  A  V  V  K
```

Question 3

```
G  R  Y  R  Y  O  A  N  U  Y  W  A  D  Y  E  Y  U  D  I  S
D  R  T  C  X  F  F  F  D  K  K  P  F  B  Q  L  O  G  N  C
H  L  E  W  Z  K  C  T  M  U  T  T  M  C  D  V  B  N  H  Y
H  B  F  B  P  X  K  S  M  O  V  T  E  V  B  V  Z  M  E  Y
A  Y  A  Q  P  K  O  T  I  K  S  C  X  F  D  K  P  R  U  S
B  O  S  Z  J  K  J  S  T  E  H  T  Y  X  J  C  O  G  M  F
Z  L  F  B  T  Q  G  B  I  Z  A  Q  L  S  K  A  M  C  N  G
V  Z  T  L  R  U  N  N  I  N  G  B  A  C  K  B  K  S  Y  R
O  H  H  R  G  A  H  B  W  D  S  X  G  U  A  R  D  M  X  Y
V  W  J  Z  R  R  V  S  H  E  I  J  X  I  D  E  W  Q  Q  N
Y  L  D  M  R  T  W  C  V  O  A  D  R  K  N  N  X  D  A  S
O  D  L  W  D  E  E  X  B  E  E  I  H  M  F  R  K  F  Q  K
S  K  H  X  H  R  K  J  V  Y  Q  T  Q  P  G  O  T  Q  G  E
O  Z  F  M  G  B  Z  C  Q  N  R  E  T  N  E  C  X  E  P  L
V  I  F  V  Z  A  M  K  A  S  I  S  Z  B  V  T  H  R  J  K
T  A  E  K  W  C  Z  X  S  B  U  O  O  N  P  S  Z  C  B  C
X  Y  F  Z  H  K  M  Z  K  O  E  D  L  J  T  U  J  Y  N  A
R  R  E  C  E  I  V  E  R  S  N  N  K  Z  K  B  E  D  X  T
O  P  H  X  O  K  D  V  W  P  C  H  I  I  R  J  G  T  X  D
D  M  Q  H  T  C  H  N  T  T  A  T  B  L  I  G  S  S  W  D
```

1. Fumble	6. Cornerback
2. Quarterback	7. Safety
3. Receiver	8. Center
4. Running Back	9. Guard
5. Linebacker	10. Tackle

Answers

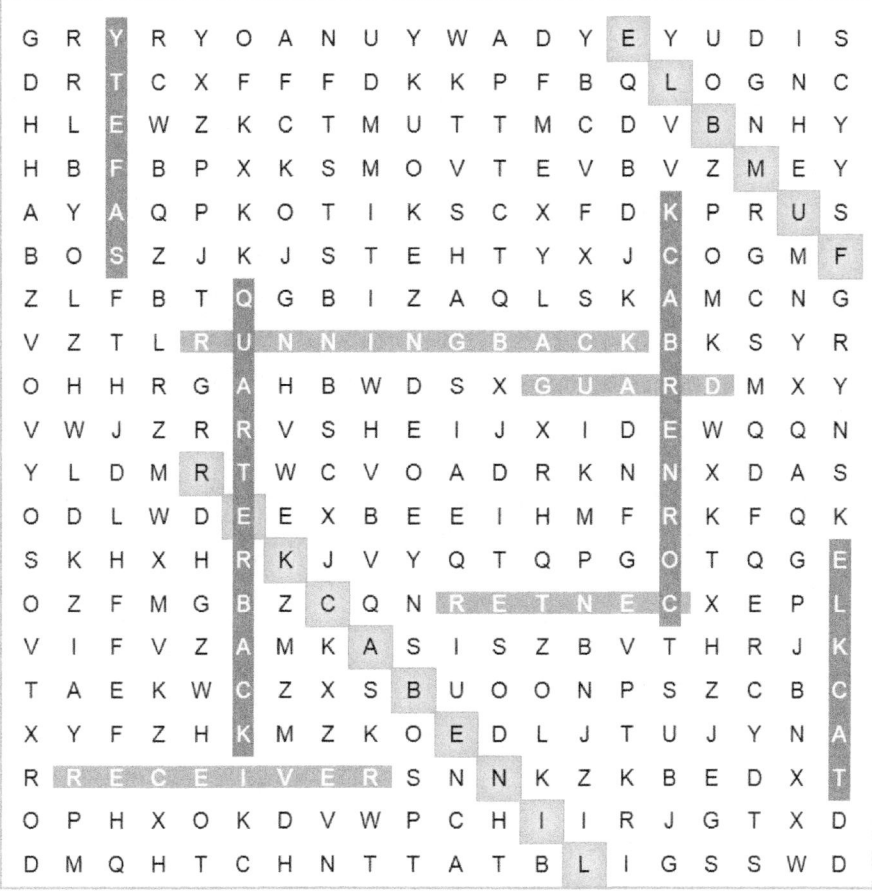

G	R	Y	R	Y	O	A	N	U	Y	W	A	D	Y	E	Y	U	D	I	S
D	R	T	C	X	F	F	F	D	K	K	P	F	B	Q	L	O	G	N	C
H	L	E	W	Z	K	C	T	M	U	T	T	M	C	D	V	B	N	H	Y
H	B	F	B	P	X	K	S	M	O	V	T	E	V	B	V	Z	M	E	Y
A	Y	A	Q	P	K	O	T	I	K	S	C	X	F	D	K	P	R	U	S
B	O	S	Z	J	K	J	S	T	E	H	T	Y	X	J	C	O	G	M	F
Z	L	F	B	T	Q	G	B	I	Z	A	Q	L	S	K	A	M	C	N	G
V	Z	T	L	R	U	N	N	I	N	G	B	A	C	K	B	K	S	Y	R
O	H	H	R	G	A	H	B	W	D	S	X	G	U	A	R	D	M	X	Y
V	W	J	Z	R	R	V	S	H	E	I	J	X	I	D	E	W	Q	Q	N
Y	L	D	M	R	T	W	C	V	O	A	D	R	K	N	N	X	D	A	S
O	D	L	W	D	E	E	X	B	E	E	I	H	M	F	R	K	F	Q	K
S	K	H	X	H	R	K	J	V	Y	Q	T	Q	P	G	O	T	Q	G	E
O	Z	F	M	G	B	Z	C	Q	N	R	E	T	N	E	C	X	E	P	L
V	I	F	V	Z	A	M	K	A	S	I	S	Z	B	V	T	H	R	J	K
T	A	E	K	W	C	Z	X	S	B	U	O	O	N	P	S	Z	C	B	C
X	Y	F	Z	H	K	M	Z	K	O	E	D	L	J	T	U	J	Y	N	A
R	R	E	C	E	I	V	E	R	S	N	N	K	Z	K	B	E	D	X	T
O	P	H	X	O	K	D	V	W	P	C	H	I	I	R	J	G	T	X	D
D	M	Q	H	T	C	H	N	T	T	A	T	B	L	I	G	S	S	W	D

115

Question 4

```
Y D I O S L L I B O L A F F U B S N F V
N R L B M U W B C L I D N M M F E A Y N
Y G A W R O X V C T Y F E C R W F O S G
R E O M L U V S T P K Z D F Y C S A T A
L F L S L C G J A L Z Y O O C R S D V O
A H E G L I S K X U W S R H Y A M L G D
V O K H L G A H X J M K A C I N A Z O A
I N M S I N O H U T J M Y P X K E D L Z
R V I B R E E I U E P E X W W F T N Y L
I K A K D V G Q T I X W M U B K L V T J
C O M N E W B S O P K C T I N O A I P O
Z G I B T J H N I N I X K F T V I C X P
B V D K U I S Y X M J O E O M R C G H J
Z I O B N H G O W U R K Z O A R E M J M
O R L N I T L H W F N Y K X K B P V L H
R S P P M E Q T T P A N V N A Q S F O W
C S H D O C F F R E D U I S G Y Z W K G
B N I B W G W H X Y N M B A C S J U L X
J U N N T R W E X E M D U N J G G M S H
T E S Z O D C O J N C Y M M B J O K Y V
```

1. Tight End
2. Special Teams
3. Hail Mary
4. Two minute Drill
5. Overtime

6. Rivalry
7. Miami Dolphins
8. New York Jets
9. Buffalo Bills
10. AFC Championship

Answers

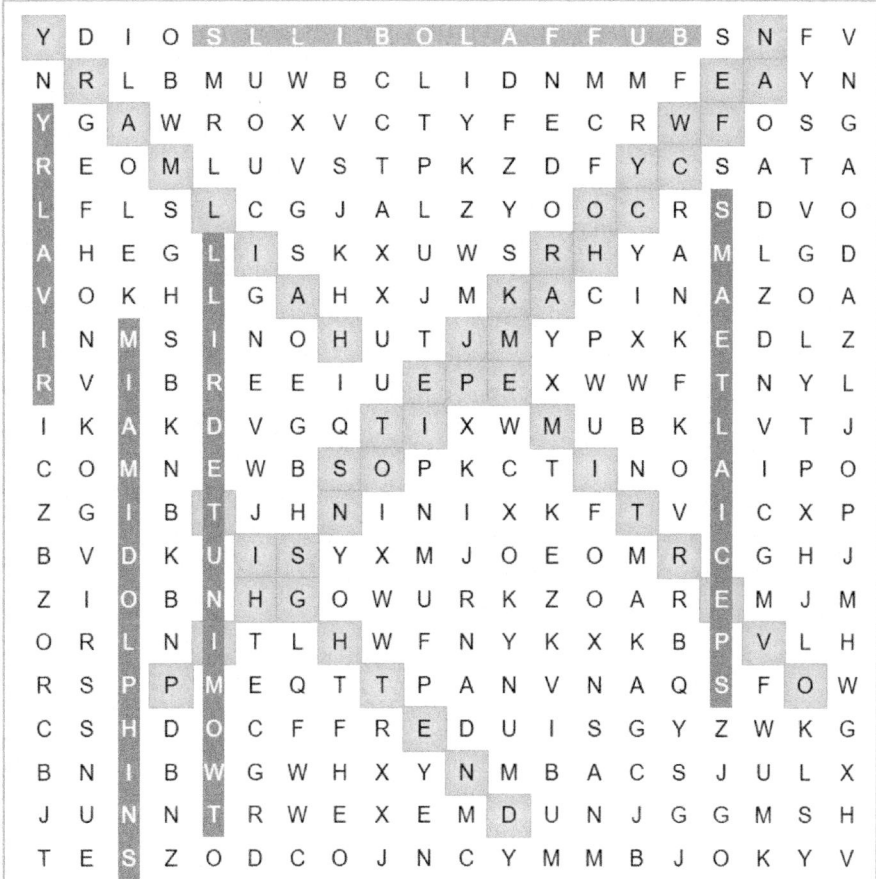

Y	D	I	O	S	L	L	I	B	O	L	A	F	F	U	B	S	N	F	V
N	R	L	B	M	U	W	B	C	L	I	D	N	M	M	F	E	A	Y	N
Y	G	A	W	R	O	X	V	C	T	Y	F	E	C	R	W	F	O	S	G
R	E	O	M	L	U	V	S	T	P	K	Z	D	F	Y	C	S	A	T	A
L	F	L	S	L	C	G	J	A	L	Z	Y	O	O	C	R	S	D	V	O
A	H	E	G	L	I	S	K	X	U	W	S	R	H	Y	A	M	L	G	D
V	O	K	H	L	G	A	H	X	J	M	K	A	C	I	N	A	Z	O	A
I	N	M	S	I	N	O	H	U	T	J	M	Y	P	X	K	E	D	L	Z
R	V	I	B	R	E	E	I	U	E	P	E	X	W	W	F	T	N	Y	L
I	K	A	K	D	V	G	Q	T	I	X	W	M	U	B	K	L	V	T	J
C	O	M	N	E	W	B	S	O	P	K	C	T	I	N	O	A	I	P	O
Z	G	I	B	T	J	H	N	I	N	I	X	K	F	T	V	I	C	X	P
B	V	D	K	U	I	S	Y	X	M	J	O	E	O	M	R	C	G	H	J
Z	I	O	B	N	H	G	O	W	U	R	K	Z	O	A	R	E	M	J	M
O	R	L	N	I	T	L	H	W	F	N	Y	K	X	K	B	P	V	L	H
R	S	P	P	M	E	Q	T	T	P	A	N	V	N	A	Q	S	F	O	W
C	S	H	D	O	C	F	F	R	E	D	U	I	S	G	Y	Z	W	K	G
B	N	I	B	W	G	W	H	X	Y	N	M	B	A	C	S	J	U	L	X
J	U	N	N	T	R	W	E	X	E	M	D	U	N	J	G	G	M	S	H
T	E	S	Z	O	D	C	O	J	N	C	Y	M	M	B	J	O	K	Y	V

117

Question 5

```
D  B  A  M  V  R  K  D  E  M  T  E  H  M  F  P  S  T  D  F
I  E  F  W  O  J  Y  I  A  W  D  C  U  I  E  B  I  I  R  J
M  X  Y  N  O  O  X  U  U  U  M  L  L  S  P  Q  V  A  D  X
J  N  N  K  O  U  J  U  O  W  Q  U  L  C  Y  I  J  O  B  K
D  C  K  O  Q  G  J  E  R  E  A  S  Z  G  S  R  U  V  I  P
I  L  J  M  N  S  R  E  R  K  Z  G  E  I  G  I  G  O  C  N
Q  I  C  G  C  K  T  A  M  C  U  S  O  C  W  G  Y  Q  P  J
U  U  R  J  O  S  C  J  P  V  Q  N  R  H  I  W  S  D  J  P
P  R  O  B  O  W  L  X  K  L  A  P  E  N  L  T  X  L  V  T
V  A  U  R  U  Z  R  V  Y  L  T  Y  G  E  D  O  C  Z  V  K
M  K  T  O  W  L  P  W  R  C  E  F  H  P  C  E  S  A  E  D
D  T  X  W  X  H  B  O  P  A  N  K  A  W  A  L  A  I  R  D
G  M  R  S  V  N  U  I  I  Z  H  E  F  R  R  O  Z  E  E  P
C  S  S  I  L  N  I  C  Y  T  T  Q  G  J  D  N  G  K  G  Y
E  T  W  V  D  W  E  X  M  U  P  N  B  A  E  I  D  M  J  A
V  D  R  N  X  H  A  L  L  O  F  F  A  M  E  W  N  B  M  X
G  S  A  K  U  I  J  U  N  G  L  N  P  J  W  E  T  O  Y  P
Q  F  Z  R  W  L  C  M  Q  V  K  K  H  P  E  H  R  O  B  K
F  Z  P  R  T  T  Y  C  Z  I  S  M  X  C  V  D  W  F  D  U
Q  I  K  U  G  D  F  U  L  X  U  Z  U  R  I  I  F  F  F  U
```

1. Wild Card	6. Draft
2. Divisional Round	7. Free Agency
3. Pro Bowl	8. Trade
4. Hall of Fame	9. Roster
5. MVP	10. Practice Squad

Answers

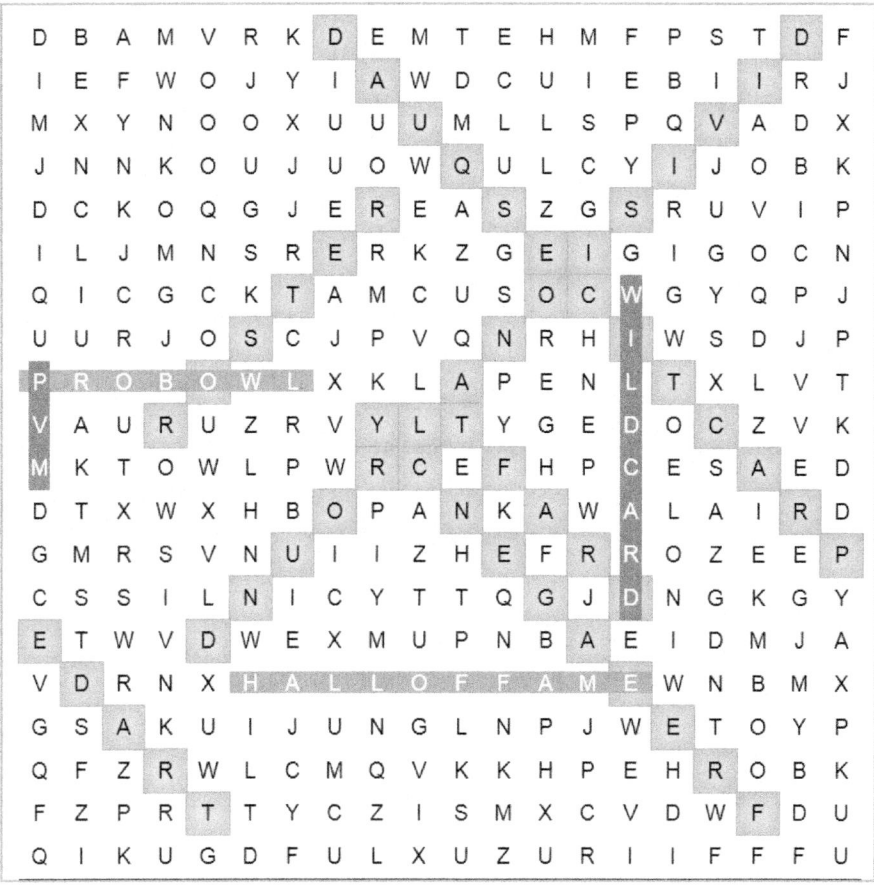

Question 6

```
S  V  Q  C  Z  G  X  R  Z  S  B  W  A  U  J  P  C  K  E  W
C  E  K  K  T  B  P  E  T  J  O  A  P  M  G  O  E  E  E  S
O  A  M  E  O  C  X  S  E  B  I  R  Q  M  H  H  U  X  T  E
D  B  U  Z  K  W  R  B  Y  L  R  O  B  M  B  C  Y  C  N  Q
S  U  Y  G  E  T  A  R  T  S  W  R  S  A  A  H  A  V  U  R
Z  L  W  J  Q  Y  A  B  F  U  Q  G  P  J  S  G  I  B  O  S
B  J  P  O  Z  V  Y  M  B  A  T  W  H  X  S  L  R  M  C  S
M  W  H  Z  R  L  O  V  Q  L  U  L  K  Z  T  I  Z  W  P  U
N  Z  T  U  S  Z  A  N  H  O  M  A  O  R  B  X  H  H  A  A
W  R  E  G  U  L  A  R  S  E  A  S  O  N  C  E  W  J  N  K
P  Y  P  Z  X  E  N  X  E  S  E  L  B  I  D  U  A  N  S  F
N  N  Q  B  N  X  Q  F  E  N  H  G  Y  I  M  X  O  B  A  P
B  R  D  S  D  O  V  Z  M  X  A  O  A  A  P  S  H  N  F  K
G  N  I  T  U  O  C  S  F  F  D  L  L  Z  A  Z  G  G  X  Q
Z  C  P  O  S  T  S  E  A  S  O  N  P  E  I  M  I  M  N  Q
M  L  M  T  R  V  V  Q  J  G  X  R  S  E  B  D  Q  T  O  L
S  Q  H  D  A  P  F  V  V  I  V  E  T  X  M  B  Z  R  J  G
Z  Y  F  Y  H  N  J  C  E  V  R  X  O  S  F  A  U  K  Y  I
V  A  F  G  X  X  S  I  R  P  S  M  U  U  A  Q  G  O  M  N
F  T  Q  K  O  O  R  P  M  A  C  G  N  I  N  I  A  R  T  L
```

1. Scouting	6. Playbook
2. Training Camp	7. Strategy
3. Preseason	8. Game Plan
4. Regular Season	9. Audibles
5. Postseason	10. Snap Count

Answers

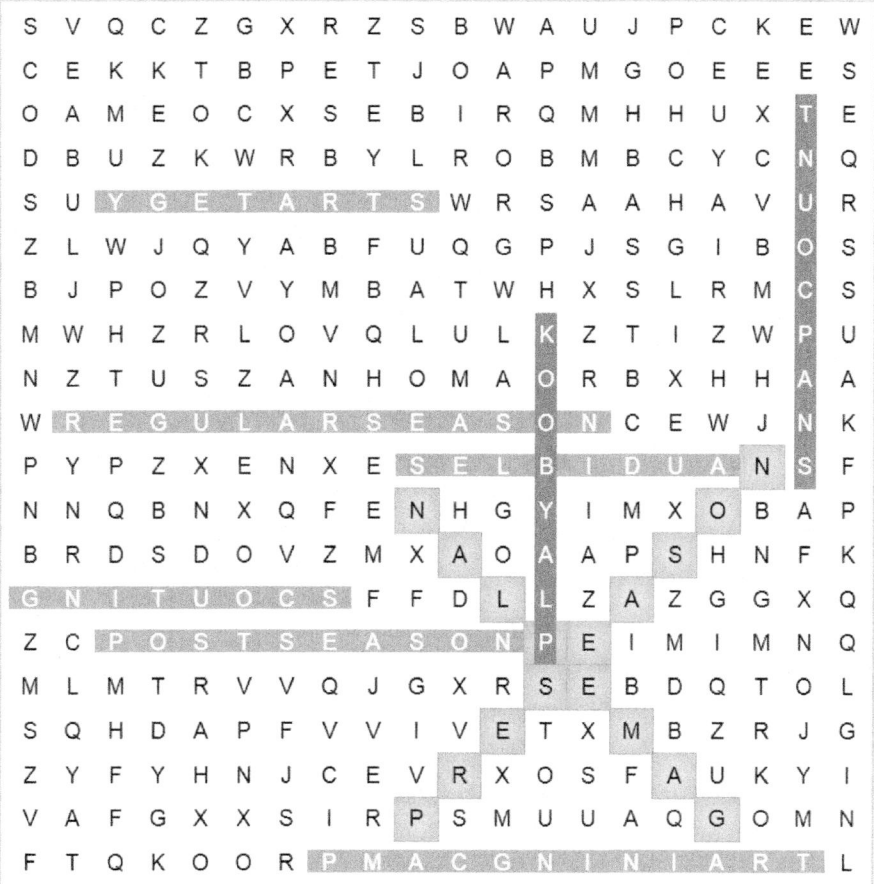

Question 7

```
T  J  Q  X  T  O  S  L  T  C  M  G  X  U  H  U  T  O  T  R
S  E  N  I  L  E  D  I  S  B  R  L  J  M  J  A  N  K  B  D
S  K  P  R  N  Q  J  B  N  E  S  I  J  P  W  T  T  E  C  C
O  G  X  E  B  E  N  O  Z  D  N  E  J  J  F  D  W  N  J  A
J  P  C  E  X  K  R  G  G  R  Y  G  E  U  Y  Y  I  L  G  Q
T  P  O  T  W  G  W  R  Q  M  E  T  B  R  D  B  E  Q  E  Z
K  R  Z  S  V  Q  I  O  H  A  J  P  T  K  E  I  Q  P  Q  S
B  D  C  H  A  L  L  E  N  G  E  F  L  A  G  F  Z  J  T  A
M  Z  A  E  K  Y  Q  Q  J  Q  H  W  T  J  F  E  E  M  U  L
R  F  I  T  R  X  P  C  C  B  B  H  E  O  T  K  U  R  V  F
C  K  R  O  Y  P  E  S  K  D  P  O  K  I  E  N  X  C  U  Z
S  A  P  U  M  T  Z  N  Y  M  N  C  M  Y  V  E  S  B  R  A
P  S  L  C  T  D  X  J  G  A  I  E  K  Y  D  E  B  N  T  Z
B  E  J  H  T  E  C  P  V  K  O  C  J  V  W  V  R  R  F  I
A  T  F  B  R  E  J  K  Z  U  P  S  Z  D  O  O  S  U  V  R
U  L  O  A  E  M  L  O  T  T  C  D  F  C  W  Y  O  T  S  P
W  Y  G  C  W  L  Y  Q  E  F  H  K  O  S  Q  P  R  E  G  L
K  U  T  K  R  G  M  O  S  U  P  U  Y  N  E  U  I  R  M  O
K  A  U  E  O  V  S  A  L  J  S  Z  X  K  C  N  E  N  T  C
G  C  C  G  H  B  D  J  F  V  J  C  J  X  Z  T  Z  L  Y  J
```

1. Timeout	6. Kickoff
2. Review	7. Punt
3. Challenge Flag	8. Return
4. Referees	9. End Zone
5. Touchback	10. Sidelines

Answers

```
T  J  Q  X  T  O  S  L  T  C  M  G  X  U  H  U  T  O  T  R
S  E  N  I  L  E  D  I  S  B  R  L  J  M  J  A  N  K  B  D
S  K  P  R  N  Q  J  B  N  E  S  I  J  P  W  T  T  E  C  C
O  G  X  E  B  E  N  O  Z  D  N  E  J  J  F  D  W  N  J  A
J  P  C  E  X  K  R  G  G  R  Y  G  E  U  Y  Y  I  L  G  Q
T  P  O  T  W  G  W  R  Q  M  E  T  B  R  D  B  E  Q  E  Z
K  R  Z  S  V  Q  I  O  H  A  J  P  T  K  E  I  Q  P  Q  S
B  D  C  H  A  L  L  E  N  G  E  F  L  A  G  F  Z  J  T  A
M  Z  A  E  K  Y  Q  Q  J  Q  H  W  T  J  F  E  E  M  U  L
R  F  I  T  R  X  P  C  C  B  B  H  E  O  T  K  U  R  V  F
C  K  R  O  Y  P  E  S  K  D  P  O  K  I  E  N  X  C  U  Z
S  A  P  U  M  T  Z  N  Y  M  N  C  M  Y  V  E  S  B  R  A
P  S  L  C  T  D  X  J  G  A  I  E  K  Y  D  E  B  N  T  Z
B  E  J  H  T  E  C  P  V  K  O  C  J  V  W  V  R  R  F  I
A  T  F  B  R  E  J  K  Z  U  P  S  Z  D  O  O  S  U  V  R
U  L  O  A  E  M  L  O  T  T  C  D  F  C  W  Y  O  T  S  P
W  Y  G  C  W  L  Y  Q  E  F  H  K  O  S  Q  P  R  E  G  L
K  U  T  K  R  G  M  O  S  U  P  U  Y  N  E  U  I  R  M  O
K  A  U  E  O  V  S  A  L  J  S  Z  X  K  C  N  E  N  T  C
G  C  C  G  H  B  D  J  F  V  J  C  J  X  Z  T  Z  L  Y  J
```

Question 8

```
E  Q  S  C  G  R  Z  Q  A  A  J  O  N  U  C  H  T  U  Z  V
T  W  S  M  Q  S  Z  R  U  G  C  Z  C  L  L  A  P  T  P  R
C  T  W  E  V  B  A  Q  T  K  U  N  Y  K  I  Y  F  F  N  L
H  O  S  R  I  A  C  Q  U  R  Y  G  G  L  N  T  O  L  D  W
O  R  B  C  R  H  D  F  A  K  R  V  G  K  S  S  H  B  N  L
X  J  K  H  L  S  P  A  D  Y  H  A  A  U  H  A  K  X  B  K
B  H  B  A  N  E  S  O  L  Y  T  W  P  C  P  N  Y  J  B  D
V  O  K  N  H  Z  G  J  R  I  X  E  H  Y  C  Y  R  K  S  P
K  H  C  D  V  Z  U  B  N  T  R  E  G  A  K  D  K  A  S  O
Z  W  A  I  U  D  E  G  Z  B  K  T  D  X  B  M  Z  E  E  H
R  P  B  S  H  S  A  O  O  D  A  M  B  E  Z  F  R  R  S  X
Y  C  E  I  F  U  O  W  T  I  L  A  X  B  S  C  Q  T  B  Q
Z  M  M  N  G  N  L  J  L  M  L  R  N  V  E  A  I  S  P  G
J  U  O  G  U  R  Z  B  J  M  U  Q  X  X  N  K  B  G  V  C
M  C  C  P  I  H  S  N  O  I  P  M  A  H  C  R  V  N  M  E
S  H  I  N  D  H  Q  S  K  V  W  A  S  I  R  N  S  I  A  E
B  E  G  E  X  K  I  D  K  B  N  Y  A  X  A  S  H  N  Z  F
C  S  U  M  W  T  F  G  Z  K  E  M  V  E  S  W  M  N  S  R
O  B  H  S  S  I  N  H  S  O  P  Z  U  S  J  C  U  I  C  N
U  U  I  Q  O  M  O  O  R  R  E  K  C  O  L  Y  K  W  T  F
```

1. Locker Room	6. Trophies
2. Fan Base	7. Championship
3. Merchandising	8. Dynasty
4. Tailgating	9. Winning Streak
5. Super Bowl Rings	10. Comeback

Answers

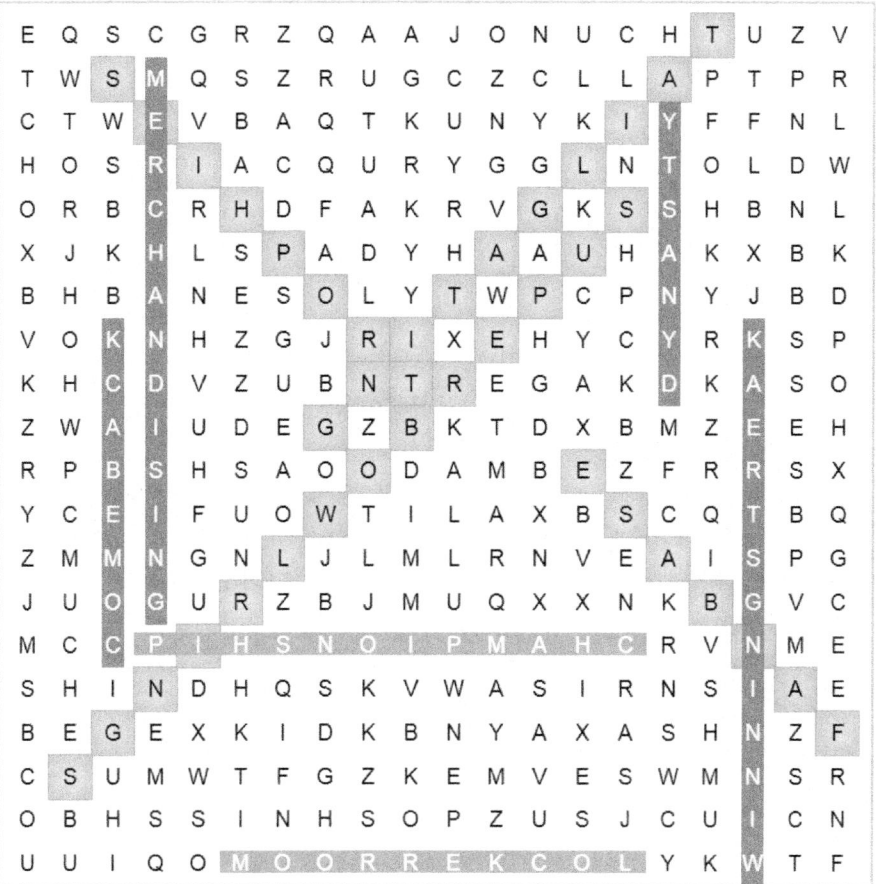

Question 9

```
H  O  M  N  M  Q  H  O  A  S  Y  S  I  R  H  W  Z  Q  W  M
S  K  P  I  L  Q  N  A  E  B  T  Z  H  A  D  L  U  N  M  B
S  H  W  V  F  I  B  N  E  L  Q  L  Q  I  W  N  R  B  Z  W
Y  B  M  G  O  P  X  T  S  U  P  N  F  O  T  F  I  V  T  Y
C  O  M  M  U  N  I  T  Y  S  E  R  V  I  C  E  C  G  G  Z
C  Z  L  U  N  N  R  Z  J  P  C  F  U  C  F  Q  X  J  Z  N
A  V  X  C  D  O  D  I  T  O  V  Z  Y  E  C  M  Y  O  M  V
N  K  T  H  A  Y  F  C  U  R  R  H  R  M  R  P  M  B  K  N
A  J  H  B  T  X  L  L  H  T  R  T  J  V  D  Q  G  I  P  U
L  U  Y  T  I  R  A  H  C  S  F  H  D  S  R  O  Z  N  A  S
Y  J  O  Q  O  F  O  S  Y  M  V  A  A  H  O  N  E  W  C  L
S  E  S  F  N  K  G  T  B  A  M  V  U  Y  C  R  K  I  E  Q
I  M  A  R  P  D  L  H  F  N  Z  X  T  W  E  D  T  D  R  L
S  O  O  E  X  M  L  G  Z  S  S  R  O  K  R  S  I  U  E  V
U  S  R  I  I  D  T  I  Y  H  W  N  G  Z  I  V  X  V  M  T
N  M  U  F  Z  S  L  L  W  I  R  B  R  T  M  I  K  X  A  O
J  S  S  K  Z  X  N  H  D  P  S  R  A  W  P  M  B  O  G  J
S  B  Q  C  K  W  U  G  R  X  N  T  P  S  C  L  H  U  W  F
W  S  V  O  L  L  R  I  J  O  S  O  H  L  Q  P  G  F  G  F
Y  B  E  S  F  W  U  H  M  H  K  M  D  H  G  T  I  L  B  W
```

1. Record	6. Sportsmanship
2. Statistics	7. Community Service
3. Highlights	8. Charity
4. Game Recap	9. Foundation
5. Analysis	10. Autograph

Answers

Question 10

I	U	Z	D	Z	F	X	Z	Y	N	I	V	R	P	U	V	O	W	Z	P
N	P	E	L	B	I	V	L	A	P	N	O	E	E	C	B	C	L	W	O
D	S	T	E	Z	U	S	F	U	J	A	M	T	U	O	X	T	J	Z	L
O	P	W	I	H	P	H	P	O	Z	I	A	R	T	S	W	A	Z	S	A
O	O	T	F	K	N	U	K	T	V	G	C	O	N	L	L	I	P	C	I
R	R	C	S	T	D	Z	Q	I	P	P	D	P	H	Y	N	L	A	W	G
S	T	T	S	H	Z	Y	A	Z	Q	R	F	E	M	I	R	G	C	W	Y
T	S	T	A	J	O	F	Q	X	J	C	V	R	U	Q	U	A	G	P	E
A	N	E	R	P	K	G	Z	W	Y	H	R	E	E	B	J	T	G	L	S
D	E	R	G	D	S	T	E	K	C	I	T	N	O	S	A	E	S	G	R
I	T	F	R	U	T	L	A	I	C	I	F	I	T	R	A	P	Q	X	E
U	W	I	R	H	O	Q	S	D	F	V	A	L	S	L	A	A	I	V	J
M	O	F	J	W	M	B	N	M	H	D	U	E	Z	Y	D	R	K	F	U
M	R	I	U	Q	J	R	X	G	E	D	A	D	I	H	N	T	T	G	I
W	K	Y	X	U	V	A	T	L	I	T	W	I	H	B	A	Y	P	F	S
K	L	X	F	N	O	Q	V	G	W	F	C	S	G	R	R	Y	S	T	C
U	C	Q	O	X	Z	M	U	I	D	A	T	S	R	O	O	D	T	U	O
P	Y	A	H	W	J	C	V	O	D	V	A	C	G	R	F	K	D	H	W
U	D	S	L	Y	M	C	N	H	M	E	M	O	R	A	B	I	L	I	A
D	E	D	E	T	E	Z	N	G	T	W	A	Y	J	W	K	Q	E	H	G

1. Memorabilia	6. Indoor Stadium
2. Jersey	7. Artificial Turf
3. Season Tickets	8. Grass Field
4. Tailgate Party	9. Sideline Reporter
5. Outdoor Stadium	10. Sports Network

Answers

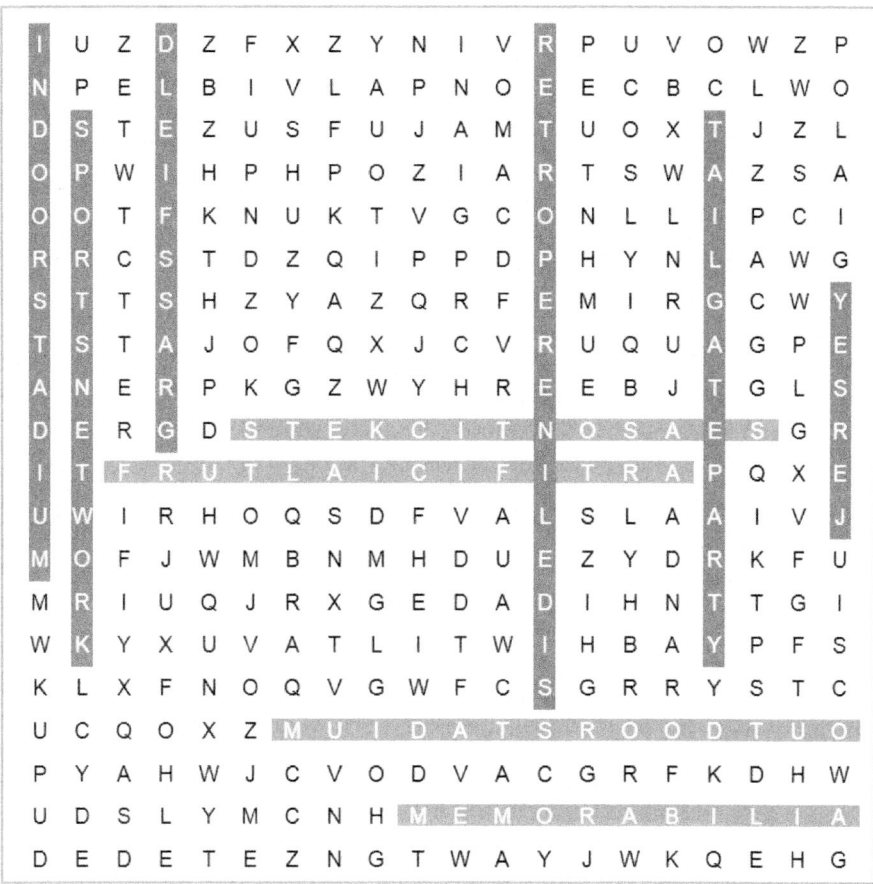

```
I U Z D Z F X Z Y N I V R P U V O W Z P
N P E L B I V L A P N O E E C B C L W O
D S T E Z U S F U J A M T U O X T J Z L
O P W I H P H P O Z I A R T S W A Z S A
O T F K N U K T V G C O N L L I P C I
R R C S T D Z Q I P P D P H Y N L A W G
S T T H Z Y A Z Q R F E M I R G C W Y
T S T A J O F Q X J C V R U Q U A G P E
A N E R P K G Z W Y H R E E B J T G L S
D E R G D S T E K C I T N O S A E S G R
I T F R U T L A I C I F I T R A P Q X E
U W I R H O Q S D F V A L S L A A I V J
M O F J W M B N M H D U E Z Y D R K F U
M R I U Q J R X G E D A D I H N T T G I
W K Y X U V A T L I T W I H B A Y P F S
K L X F N O Q V G W F C S G R R Y S T C
U C Q O X Z M U I D A T S R O O D T U O
P Y A H W J C V O D V A C G R F K D H W
U D S L Y M C N H M E M O R A B I L I A
D E D E T E Z N G T W A Y J W K Q E H G
```

Question 11

```
P  C  K  Z  U  C  Z  J  I  R  W  T  C  O  P  J  A  E  K  O
K  V  N  L  F  C  I  A  I  J  G  G  T  H  B  H  F  N  J  L
I  Q  A  L  Z  H  V  X  P  E  L  B  D  L  C  D  S  J  E  X
U  S  U  A  Q  X  T  B  L  R  D  T  L  Z  Z  R  M  V  M  W
J  U  R  B  W  I  V  G  U  K  P  S  E  B  J  E  R  B  I  N
D  P  U  T  H  X  B  D  R  W  S  S  T  Z  C  S  F  D  B  F
H  E  H  O  P  B  Z  O  T  I  X  T  S  A  C  D  A  O  R  B
S  R  R  O  Z  M  N  X  E  N  I  Z  S  R  F  D  Q  J  V  P
P  B  W  F  A  W  P  T  B  A  Y  G  Y  R  T  O  S  Y  J  G
H  O  N  Y  W  I  L  T  V  D  W  X  J  T  S  G  K  T  T  L
Q  W  U  S  F  M  D  U  A  M  N  I  J  R  A  N  T  I  Z  J
F  L  U  A  H  A  K  E  L  G  G  U  E  T  C  I  D  O  I  F
Z  X  Y  T  Z  G  P  D  M  Z  O  E  X  H  D  T  C  X  R  J
U  X  W  N  G  Q  T  Q  L  L  T  C  N  J  O  T  E  W  H  M
X  X  V  A  O  F  F  I  C  I  A  L  A  P  P  E  E  P  I  W
Z  V  H  F  J  C  U  G  S  A  H  I  O  K  W  B  N  I  C  B
M  I  P  M  N  R  D  B  O  E  B  I  C  I  G  B  D  L  L  C
U  Z  T  Q  C  M  E  I  O  N  D  R  G  O  Q  R  W  M  P  K
M  C  W  Z  H  W  P  V  S  A  T  Q  J  A  S  O  X  P  M  O
Z  E  I  L  L  W  O  B  R  E  P  U  S  N  F  J  G  C  L  M
```

1. Broadcast	6. Official App
2. Radio	7. Fantasy Football
3. Podcast	8. Betting Odds
4. Social Media	9. Super Bowl LI
5. Website	10. Super Bowl XXXVI

Answers

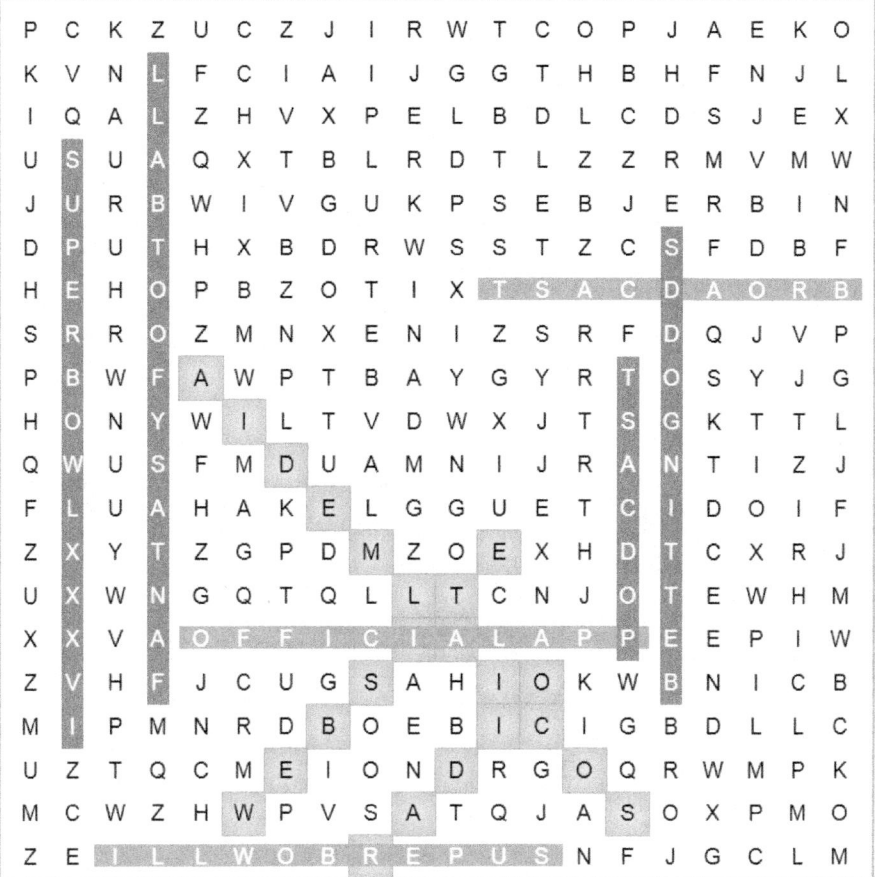

Question 12

```
J  Q  E  V  I  R  D  G  N  I  N  N  I  W  E  M  A  G  N  B
D  P  L  Q  1  6  0  S  E  A  S  O  N  T  S  X  G  R  T  L
Y  U  M  B  O  A  S  S  A  P  N  W  O  D  H  C  U  O  T  W
R  K  Y  P  C  O  M  E  B  A  C  K  W  I  N  P  U  L  F  W
S  C  J  L  M  P  X  Q  A  N  M  L  Y  M  L  G  Z  C  M  Q
P  K  R  L  L  A  S  T  M  I  N  U  T  E  W  I  N  B  F  W
A  I  F  V  S  K  Q  E  I  R  K  M  B  L  C  Q  P  T  K  E
D  C  L  U  T  C  H  P  E  R  F  O  R  M  A  N  C  E  G  N
J  E  X  J  T  S  U  P  E  R  B  O  W  L  L  I  I  I  U  P
A  S  H  U  C  I  S  G  Y  J  C  I  G  T  B  Q  N  A  N  M
I  F  X  I  L  X  L  W  O  B  R  E  P  U  S  N  G  B  D  J
P  V  L  B  M  T  H  V  A  B  W  Y  E  Q  T  N  Q  I  E  L
I  I  I  V  X  X  X  L  W  O  B  R  E  P  U  S  I  P  F  E
R  S  D  H  X  K  T  F  B  Y  A  P  M  V  R  Z  W  C  E  Z
W  Y  I  V  D  H  F  O  F  J  H  H  D  V  F  J  K  O  A  K
G  H  N  T  P  X  S  Y  V  Q  D  O  V  W  Z  R  H  S  T  A
U  E  P  R  V  Z  Q  V  V  C  J  F  R  F  V  D  R  A  E  G
G  J  E  C  Q  F  M  M  H  Z  E  E  K  B  M  G  Y  G  D  U
H  H  B  G  U  Q  D  X  U  U  T  W  X  X  D  U  L  R  X  O
O  P  A  J  K  W  W  R  K  A  C  U  I  J  Z  A  N  J  F  J
```

1. Super Bowl XXXVIII	6. Comeback Win
2. Super Bowl XLIX	7. Last-Minute Win
3. Super Bowl LIII	8. Clutch Performance
4. 16-0 Season	9. Game-winning Drive
5. Undefeated	10. Touchdown Pass

Answers

```
J  Q  E  V  I  R  D  G  N  I  N  N  I  W  E  M  A  G  N  B
D  P  L  Q  1  6  0  S  E  A  S  O  N  T  S  X  G  R  T  L
Y  U  M  B  O  A  S  S  A  P  N  W  O  D  H  C  U  O  T  W
R  K  Y  P  C  O  M  E  B  A  C  K  W  I  N  P  U  L  F  W
S  C  J  L  M  P  X  Q  A  N  M  L  Y  M  L  G  Z  C  M  Q
P  K  R  L  L  A  S  T  M  I  N  U  T  E  W  I  N  B  F  W
A  I  F  V  S  K  Q  E  I  R  K  M  B  L  C  Q  P  T  K  E
D  C  L  U  T  C  H  P  E  R  F  O  R  M  A  N  C  E  G  N
J  E  X  J  T  S  U  P  E  R  B  O  W  L  L  I  I  I  U  P
A  S  H  U  C  I  S  G  Y  J  C  I  G  T  B  Q  N  A  N  M
I  F  X  I  L  X  L  W  O  B  R  E  P  U  S  N  G  B  D  J
P  V  L  B  M  T  H  V  A  B  W  Y  E  Q  T  N  Q  I  E  L
I  I  I  V  X  X  X  L  W  O  B  R  E  P  U  S  I  P  F  E
R  S  D  H  X  K  T  F  B  Y  A  P  M  V  R  Z  W  C  E  Z
W  Y  I  V  D  H  F  O  F  J  H  H  D  V  F  J  K  O  A  K
G  H  N  T  P  X  S  Y  V  Q  D  O  V  W  Z  R  H  S  T  A
U  E  P  R  V  Z  Q  V  V  C  J  F  R  F  V  D  R  A  E  G
G  J  E  C  Q  F  M  M  H  Z  E  E  K  B  M  G  Y  G  D  U
H  H  B  G  U  Q  D  X  U  U  T  W  X  X  D  U  L  R  X  O
O  P  A  J  K  W  W  R  K  A  C  U  I  J  Z  A  N  J  F  J
```

Question 13

```
O  E  L  B  E  U  J  F  M  H  B  F  E  I  E  T  S  P  Q  E
O  Q  W  W  K  S  H  H  B  L  N  N  J  X  V  K  A  R  G  W
O  L  D  K  E  N  I  L  E  V  I  S  N  E  F  E  D  W  O  O
Q  I  C  R  D  P  K  Z  E  L  M  N  F  W  W  S  A  V  Q  U
C  Z  M  B  O  D  S  V  E  Q  W  N  J  L  I  E  N  W  D  Z
O  Y  O  M  R  C  F  V  X  V  Y  B  O  R  Y  D  K  X  B  M
V  H  I  Z  W  U  I  J  U  B  P  W  I  Q  Y  V  W  C  P  F
Z  G  Q  L  T  S  S  C  P  P  T  K  N  M  G  S  Y  Z  J  F
J  R  A  Q  N  I  U  H  V  K  X  P  N  K  J  D  B  S  M  J
J  C  S  E  K  C  L  S  I  E  Z  P  C  I  R  R  Y  C  A  B
X  W  F  A  J  R  S  B  P  N  R  K  I  M  A  A  C  L  O  V
T  F  Q  I  F  C  R  Z  O  O  G  T  Y  V  J  Y  R  H  I  W
O  R  P  O  Q  E  A  K  T  N  Q  Y  T  Y  B  G  T  S  V  H
H  N  D  T  X  R  T  C  N  G  A  S  A  H  E  N  Z  N  N  Y
C  T  Y  M  U  N  Y  Y  B  J  Y  Z  C  R  V  I  Q  T  D  E
U  S  C  R  E  E  N  P  A  S  S  S  E  E  D  S  A  C  K  P
X  D  Z  Y  T  L  T  O  T  A  L  Y  A  R  D  S  I  N  F  K
M  Y  R  J  N  O  I  T  C  A  Y  A  L  P  N  A  Z  Q  H  X
C  I  W  L  R  S  P  H  X  W  G  Z  F  A  I  P  X  D  A  K
T  V  Q  C  S  T  X  X  O  H  U  H  Y  H  Z  E  Z  Q  X  X
```

1. Rushing Yards	6. Play Action
2. Passing Yards	7. Screen Pass
3. Total Yards	8. Blitz
4. Defensive Line	9. Sack
5. Offensive Line	10. Safety

Answers

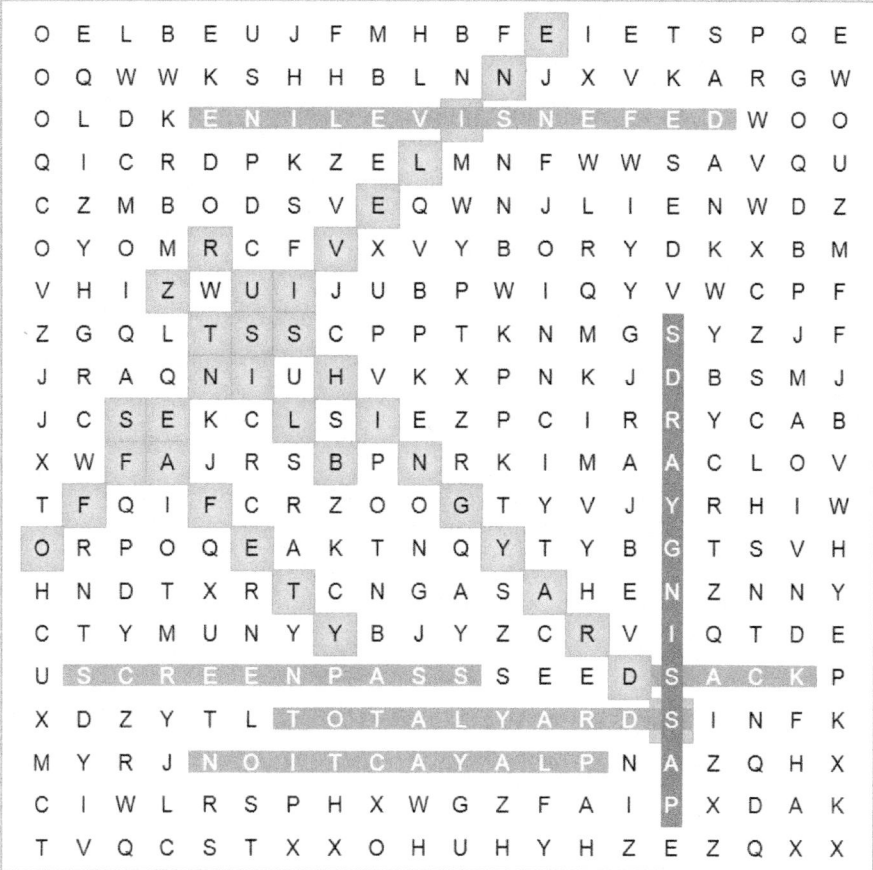

O E L B E U J F M H B F **E** I E T S P Q E
O Q W W K S H H B L N **N** J X V K A R G W
O L D K **E N I L E V I S N E F E D** W O O
Q I C R D P K Z E **L** M N F W W S A V Q U
C Z M B O D S V **E** Q W N J L I E N W D Z
O Y O M **R** C F **V** X V Y B O R Y D K X B M
V H I **Z** W **U** **I** J U B P W I Q Y V W C P F
Z G Q L **T** **S** **S** C P P T K N M G **S** Y Z J F
J R A Q **N** **I** **U** **H** V K X P N K J **D** B S M J
J C **S** E K C **L** **S** **I** E Z P C I R **R** Y C A B
X W **F** A J R S **B** P **N** R K I M A **A** C L O V
T **F** Q I **F** C R Z O O **G** T Y V J **Y** R H I W
O R P O Q **E** A K T N Q **Y** T Y B **G** T S V H
H N D T X **R** **T** C N G A S **A** H E **N** Z N N Y
C T Y M U N Y **Y** B J Y Z C **R** V **I** Q T D E
U **S C R E E N P A S S** S E E D **S A C K** P
X D Z Y T L **T O T A L Y A R D S** I N F K
M Y R J **N O I T C A Y A L P** N **A** Z Q H X
C I W L R S P H X W G Z F A I **P** X D A K
T V Q C S T X X O H U H Y H Z E Z Q X X

135

Question 14

```
G  L  B  G  S  M  Y  D  E  L  A  Y  O  F  G  A  M  E  A  R
S  C  Z  M  S  Y  T  L  A  N  E  P  M  Y  K  G  F  T  W  E
W  R  W  P  D  O  T  Z  G  A  N  V  W  N  Z  C  C  B  C  Z
G  C  C  R  K  C  U  X  C  L  J  J  P  Y  Y  X  K  N  X  F
N  O  I  T  A  M  R  O  F  L  A  G  E  L  L  I  E  P  C  B
A  Y  L  A  X  W  N  N  M  Q  W  A  J  H  U  R  E  U  F  Z
S  X  V  Q  Q  L  O  H  Q  G  L  J  O  X  E  Q  K  U  D  X
I  O  E  S  G  R  V  R  Q  F  E  L  D  F  E  G  H  U  Y  F
P  B  K  X  P  K  E  P  F  M  D  F  R  D  W  M  T  D  L  I
N  V  D  U  T  M  R  F  U  I  V  E  I  I  M  F  Z  V  Y  R
A  Z  F  A  F  R  F  O  N  N  T  S  N  V  R  R  V  M  Z  I
L  P  P  Y  R  A  A  G  N  N  F  E  T  O  S  T  Z  Y  N  D
Z  S  V  T  X  X  L  P  I  F  K  Z  R  N  J  F  I  Z  E  A
B  P  N  H  P  E  R  S  O  N  A  L  F  O  U  L  N  X  B  L
U  Z  K  Q  C  P  S  U  E  I  H  J  J  I  H  V  N  W  C  E
I  P  U  T  N  A  I  V  U  S  N  L  R  F  T  Y  E  Z  F  S
T  W  P  O  P  P  H  I  Q  Q  T  T  K  B  V  Y  B  L  L  T
Q  D  Z  A  Q  G  L  F  O  C  M  A  E  O  Y  K  H  O  F  R
D  G  G  C  X  C  Z  Y  I  Z  Z  I  R  S  C  N  E  W  I  Q
U  I  X  Q  G  H  O  L  A  L  A  J  Z  T  N  O  K  O  O  W
```

1. Turnover	6. Delay of Game
2. Penalty	7. Illegal Formation
3. Personal Foul	8. Offside
4. Pass Interference	9. False Start
5. Holding	10. Extra Point

Answers

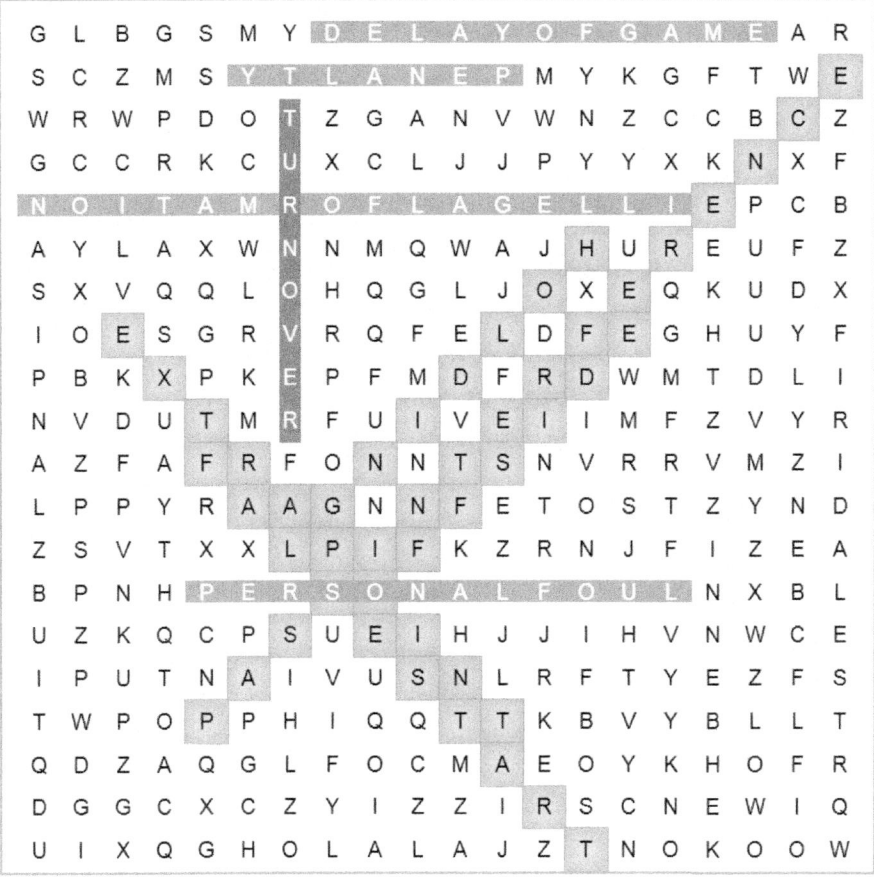

Question 15

```
A  K  M  V  S  W  Q  N  U  E  M  A  G  E  R  P  W  U  C  V
W  P  X  A  Y  B  D  T  K  N  Q  Z  U  K  H  F  H  Y  I  F
R  Z  A  T  D  W  F  T  J  R  K  B  A  Q  U  L  J  E  Y  K
G  E  Z  M  N  Q  V  O  P  R  B  P  R  Z  R  G  K  Y  I  O
V  E  X  Q  W  N  O  V  G  V  S  E  D  P  Y  R  S  Y  Q  P
V  B  A  N  Z  P  N  M  E  H  C  G  O  A  L  L  I  N  E  F
F  M  D  L  I  L  S  T  A  N  D  S  W  M  K  N  G  K  X  F
C  C  A  W  P  Q  K  M  T  H  Z  O  N  P  T  O  E  J  F  N
N  H  F  A  I  R  C  A  T  C  H  S  N  I  S  L  W  G  L  K
P  W  O  V  A  A  Q  V  N  S  R  C  P  E  B  R  X  R  T  K
A  Q  O  E  N  O  Z  D  E  R  B  Y  T  F  V  K  P  A  J  E
E  G  J  D  H  D  W  M  D  F  A  N  C  H  A  N  T  D  Z  A
T  M  B  I  H  Q  I  I  Y  R  S  M  A  S  O  K  I  Y  D  M
B  M  M  E  H  T  N  A  L  A  N  O  I  T  A  N  Y  B  S  L
W  X  F  I  F  V  R  T  C  D  E  H  P  P  M  T  W  J  K  F
H  P  A  L  Y  J  P  U  M  X  Z  U  S  T  Y  D  T  G  Z  S
B  U  A  S  D  A  Y  Y  O  S  N  R  U  T  E  R  T  N  U  P
R  H  X  Z  L  R  M  V  N  F  T  Z  O  C  H  Q  T  Y  J  Z
E  U  X  M  H  E  N  L  N  S  C  X  S  S  L  O  S  T  I  L
K  I  C  K  R  E  T  U  R  N  A  L  S  L  I  B  R  V  J  U
```

1. Red Zone	6. Fair Catch
2. Goal Line Stand	7. Fan Chant
3. Fourth Down	8. Pregame
4. Kick Return	9. Halftime Show
5. Punt Return	10. National Anthem

Answers

```
A K M V S W Q N U E M A G E R P W U C V
W P X A Y B D T K N Q Z U K H F H Y I F
R Z A T D W F T J R K B A Q U L J E Y K
G E Z M N Q V O P R B P R Z R G K Y I O
V E X Q W N O V G V S E D P Y R S Y Q P
V B A N Z P N M E H C G O A L L I N E F
F M D L I L S T A N D S W M K N G K X F
C C A W P Q K M T H Z O N P T O E J F N
N H F A I R C A T C H S N I S L W G L K
P W O V A A Q V N S R C P E B R X R T K
A Q O E N O Z D E R B Y T F V K P A J E
E G J D H D W M D F A N C H A N T D Z A
T M B I H Q I I Y R S M A S O K I Y D M
B M M E H T N A L A N O I T A N Y B S L
W X F I F V R T C D E H P P M T W J K F
H P A L Y J P U M X Z U S T Y D T G Z S
B U A S D A Y Y O S N R U T E R T N U P
R H X Z L R M V N F T Z O C H Q T Y J Z
E U X M H E N L N S C X S S L O S T I L
K I C K R E T U R N A L S L I B R V J U
```

Question 16

```
C  U  Q  P  L  A  Y  O  F  F  B  E  R  T  H  X  I  C  N  S
P  X  Y  B  W  M  O  F  L  X  J  Z  C  Y  L  T  H  V  J  Q
C  U  X  L  G  E  Q  D  G  N  I  N  O  I  T  I  D  N  O  C
T  N  H  B  T  N  S  L  Y  Q  T  V  E  U  P  D  I  I  A  N
P  I  X  M  Z  T  A  O  X  I  O  G  E  C  G  U  V  P  C  S
E  E  R  E  H  A  B  I  L  I  T  A  T  I  O  N  D  Q  T  T
B  I  Z  F  X  L  W  F  A  Y  G  A  E  E  T  Z  V  R  K  A
X  N  V  F  O  P  W  M  A  E  T  L  A  C  I  D  E  M  N  Z
S  J  V  A  F  R  K  H  H  H  H  W  I  E  B  N  R  T  B  Y
D  U  Y  T  R  E  M  B  J  L  Q  A  N  C  G  B  V  L  D  K
S  R  B  S  Y  P  V  E  N  Q  R  Y  H  T  T  X  R  P  D  H
Y  Y  C  G  K  A  P  U  W  I  K  B  H  H  O  X  T  O  J  J
K  R  H  N  L  R  J  L  P  Z  X  T  K  Y  P  O  Z  F  H  I
H  E  J  I  L  A  A  O  D  E  R  F  D  N  Z  Q  X  F  Q  V
O  P  E  N  T  T  G  J  X  A  N  O  I  T  I  R  T  U  N  Z
M  O  J  I  Q  I  D  V  I  P  K  Q  Q  X  G  B  H  H  N  V
D  R  P  A  Z  O  E  N  D  O  F  S  E  A  S  O  N  K  H  V
G  T  K  R  D  N  I  W  T  L  T  G  G  N  H  T  S  H  G  N
X  Q  C  T  X  N  A  E  G  Z  B  F  Q  Q  Y  U  U  A  N  L
B  O  L  G  G  T  T  Q  Q  B  U  D  A  C  Q  B  G  O  A  B
```

1. Playoff Berth	6. Rehabilitation
2. End of Season	7. Conditioning
3. Training Staff	8. Strength Training
4. Medical Team	9. Nutrition
5. Injury Report	10. Mental Preparation

Answers

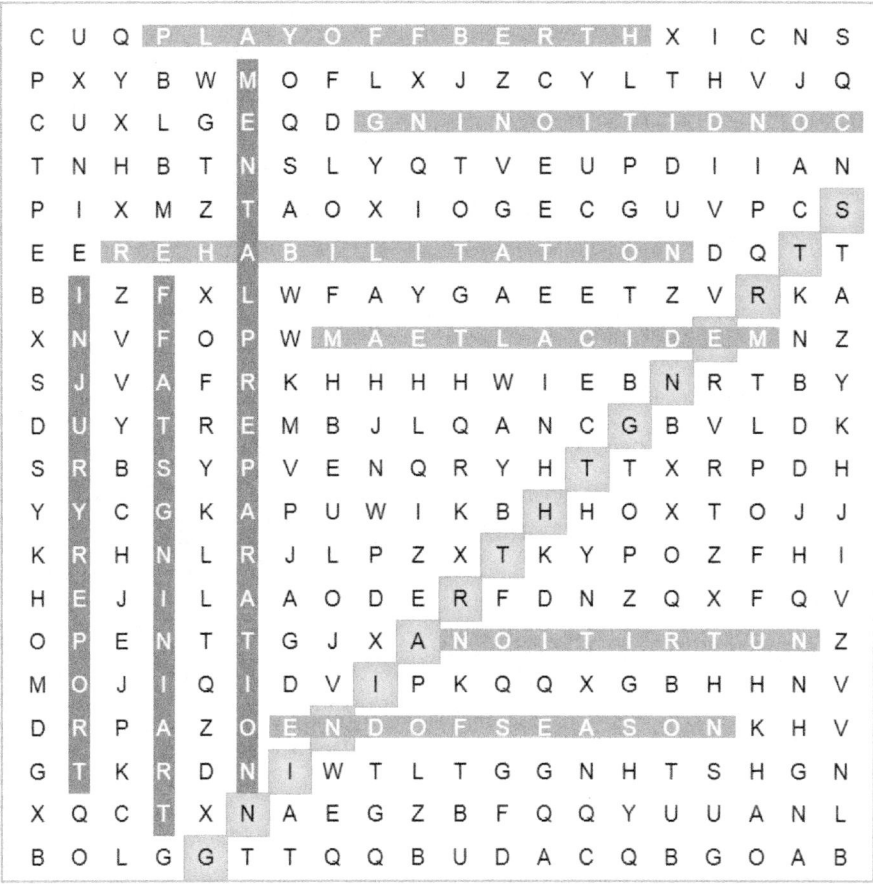

Notebook Prompt: Use this space to jot down any new facts about football you learned from this section or ideas to share with other fans. You can also jot down any questions you have about these rules or how they apply in different game situations.

....

....

....

....

....

....

....

....

....

....

....

....

....

....

....

....

CONCLUSION

The contents of this book may not be copied, reproduced or transmitted without the express written permission of the author or publisher. Under no circumstances will the publisher or author be responsible or liable for any damages, compensation or monetary loss arising from the information contained in this book, whether directly or indirectly. .

Disclaimer Notice:

Although the author and publisher have made every effort to ensure the accuracy and completeness of the content, they do not, however, make any representations or warranties as to the accuracy, completeness, or reliability of the content. , suitability or availability of the information, products, services or related graphics contained in the book for any purpose. Readers are solely responsible for their use of the information contained in this book

Every effort has been made to make this book possible. If any omission or error has occurred unintentionally, the author and publisher will be happy to acknowledge it in upcoming versions.

Printed in Dunstable, United Kingdom

68382348R00080